The Art and Craft of Whirligig Construction

Gabriel R. Zuckerman

4880 Lower Valley Road, Atglen, PA 19310 USA

Dedication

This book is dedicated to Susan, my wife, partner, and best friend. The preparation of this book has consumed a great deal of my time. I am grateful for her patience, understanding, guidance, and editorial expertise.

Contents

Copyright © 2006 by Gabriel R. Zuckerman
Library of Congress Control Number: 2005933253

Designed by Mark David Bowyer
Type set in Americana XBd BT/Souvenir Lt BT

ISBN: 0-7643-2359-8
Printed in China

Published by Schiffer Publishing Ltd.
4880 Lower Valley Road
Atglen, PA 19310
Phone: (610) 593-1777; Fax: (610) 593-2002
E-mail: Info@schifferbooks.com

For the largest selection of fine reference books on this and related subjects, please visit our web site at
www.schifferbooks.com
We are always looking for people to write books on new and related subjects. If you have an idea for a book please contact us at the above address.

This book may be purchased from the publisher.
Include $3.95 for shipping.
Please try your bookstore first.
You may write for a free catalog.

In Europe, Schiffer books are distributed by
Bushwood Books
6 Marksbury Ave.
Kew Gardens
Surrey TW9 4JF England
Phone: 44 (0) 20 8392-8585; Fax: 44 (0) 20 8392-9876
E-mail: info@bushwoodbooks.co.uk
Free postage in the U.K., Europe; air mail at cost.

Chapter 1
General Information

Introduction

The wind is an unlimited, inexhaustible, free, and valuable source of energy. It does not emit noxious fumes, or create toxic waste to pollute the environment. The wind was used by early civilizations to propel their ships for commerce, trade, and exploration. Windmills have been used to grind grain and pump water. While the wind is no longer used for these purposes, it still remains a valuable source of energy. Scientists are continuously working to develop new ways to use the wind to generate electricity. Sailboats, iceboats, and wind surfing boards require the wind to keep them in motion. Flags and banners, flapping in the wind, identify important places and call attention to special events. Weathervanes and windsocks are still used to decorate buildings and to indicate wind direction. How would children fly kites without the wind?

For hundreds of years, tinkers and handymen have been assembling scraps of material from their shops, garages, basements, and barns to create these whimsical little wind machines now called whirligigs. These craftsmen made whirligigs to pass the time and to amuse family and friends. Today, whirligigs are a recognized form of folk art. This unique and complex form of art requires the combined abilities of woodworking, metalworking, mechanics, sculpture, and painting. Whirligigs are usually made to represent contemporary activities, events or personalities, or as a visual commentary of political, social or economic issues.

I have been designing and building whirligigs for over twenty years. They are challenging to design and a joy to construct. I display one or two around the grounds of my home where they have continued to delight friends, neighbors, and visitors over the years.

The whirligig plans contained in this book represent projects that require various levels of woodworking, metalworking, and decorating skills. These whirligigs should not be confused with the garden ornaments offered by vendors at craft shows for twenty or thirty dollars. I have designed, built, and tested all of the whirligigs described. If they are carefully constructed according to my instructions, they will operate reliably for many years. Patterns, mechanical drawings, and photographs are used to illustrate construction details. Special jigs will often be required to accomplish some of the construction techniques. I have used photographs made during construction to describe these techniques. Tips to simplify some of the layout and construction are also provided where necessary. A color photograph of each whirligig in this book has been included which may be useful when painting and decorating your project. The **Parts and Materials** lists included with each project will identify the labeled items shown in the illustrations that follow.

Some of the materials and tools recommended in the book may be difficult to find. The cross-referenced appendix at the end of the book will identify the vendors of items that can be purchased by mail, telephone or on the Internet.

How It Works/
General Design

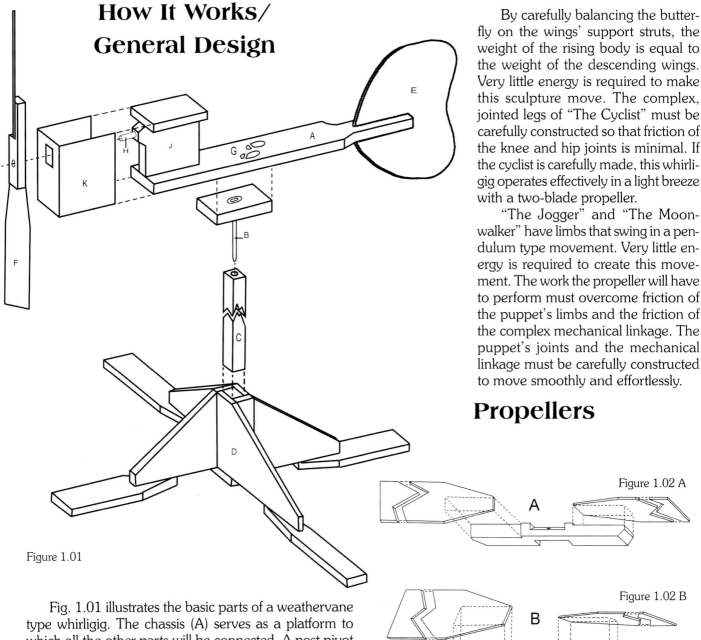

Figure 1.01

By carefully balancing the butterfly on the wings' support struts, the weight of the rising body is equal to the weight of the descending wings. Very little energy is required to make this sculpture move. The complex, jointed legs of "The Cyclist" must be carefully constructed so that friction of the knee and hip joints is minimal. If the cyclist is carefully made, this whirligig operates effectively in a light breeze with a two-blade propeller.

"The Jogger" and "The Moonwalker" have limbs that swing in a pendulum type movement. Very little energy is required to create this movement. The work the propeller will have to perform must overcome friction of the puppet's limbs and the friction of the complex mechanical linkage. The puppet's joints and the mechanical linkage must be carefully constructed to move smoothly and effortlessly.

Propellers

Figure 1.02 A

Figure 1.02 B

A propeller converts the energy of the wind into rotary mechanical motion, which is used to produce movement of the puppet sculpture. The size of the propeller required for each whirligig will depend upon the wind conditions during which it will be expected to operate and the work it will be required to perform to overcome friction and the weight of objects it will be required to move. The amount of mechanical energy a propeller can generate is directly proportional to the surface area of the blades, the number of blades, and the diameter of the propeller. The blades of the propeller should be oriented at a 45° angle to the oncoming air mass for maximum efficiency. The propellers can be modified by varying the number and size of the blades employed and the distance from the blades to the center of the hub. The

Fig. 1.01 illustrates the basic parts of a weathervane type whirligig. The chassis (A) serves as a platform to which all the other parts will be connected. A post pivot (B) allows the chassis to rotate in the horizontal plane and supports the whirligigs on top of a post (C) and stand (D). A rudder (E) keeps the propeller (F) facing into the wind. A jointed sculpture mounted on the chassis (G) creates the theme of the whirligig. The drive shaft (H) is held in the drive shaft mounting block (J) at the front end of the chassis. Any additional mechanical components mounted on the drive shaft mounting block can be concealed by a cowling (K).

The animated sculptures are constructed from wood, which has been cut to shape on a bandsaw or scroll saw and glued and screwed together and carved, to give the figures three dimensions. The parts can be carved and sculptured either partially or entirely to achieve a more realistic appearance. The sculptures should be designed so that the parts to be lifted are counterbalanced by parts of equal weight that will simultaneously descend. "Bush with a Butterfly" is an example of counterbalance.

propellers must be balanced before installation, so that they will not have to overcome a weight differential on one side of the propeller during operation. Figures 1.02 A and B illustrate propeller designs with two blades. Two of the propellers shown in Fig. 1.02 B can be made to intersect at their centers with a half lap joint to produce a four-blade propeller.

Propellers can also be made using round or polygonal hubs. By placing spokes around the perimeter of these hubs, propellers with three or more blades can be made. The front surface of the hub can be counterbored to recess the front mounting nut and washer. Fig. 1.03 illustrates the hub and spokes of a four-blade propeller. Note the kerf and eased edges on the end of the spoke that will be inserted into the hub. The measured drawing shown in Fig. 1.04 provides the layout and dimensions of the hub and spokes.

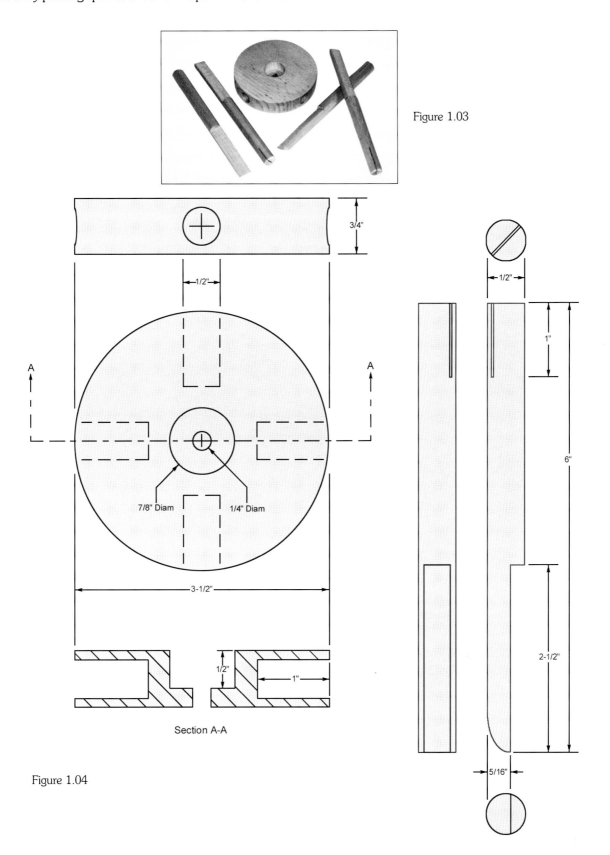

Figure 1.03

Section A-A

Figure 1.04

5

Figure 1.05

Figure 1.06

The spokes are made from short sections of a 1/2" dowel. The flat areas on the spokes are made on the bandsaw using the "V" block as shown in Fig. 1.05. Use the "V" block to make a kerf in the opposite end of the spoke to make it easier to insert the spoke into the hole in the hub. The spoke holes in the hub can be accurately drilled using a doweling jig or with a drill press and a "V" block to hold the hubs on edge. By changing the shape of the hub to a square, pentagon or hexagon, four, five or six blades can be installed on a hub. Using a round hub, any number of spoke holes can be evenly spaced around the perimeter to make a multiple blade propeller. Layout the desired number of spoke holes around the edge of the hub and drill the holes. The "V" block shown in Fig. 1.06 will accurately position a round hub in a drill press while the holes are drilled.

The propeller blades are glued and screwed to the flat areas on the spokes. The spokes are then glued into the spoke holes, with the blades oriented at a 45° angle to the propeller shaft, to produce clockwise rotation. A screw is used to hold the spoke in the correct position while the glue sets, and for additional strength. The propeller must be balanced after assembly.

The Drive Train and Mechanical Components

The drive train (Fig. 1.07), consists of all the mechanical parts between the propeller and the jointed sculpture. The drive shaft (1) is a brass rod, which is threaded on one end so that it may be connected to the propeller. The propeller is designed to rotate clockwise, as viewed from a position within the oncoming air mass. Clockwise rotation prevents the nuts, used to fasten the propeller to the right hand threads on the drive shaft,

Figure 1.07

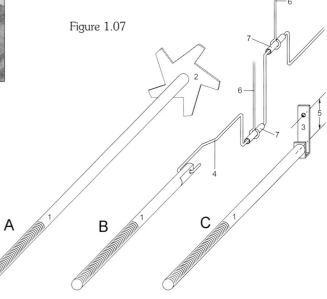

from working loose as the propeller turns. The opposite end of the drive shaft has a gear (2), crank arm (3) or is modified for connection to a crankshaft (4).

Using crank arms, crankshafts, levers, and bars, the rotation of the drive shaft is converted into the reciprocal movement used to activate the puppet sculptures. The mechanical system may be as simple as the mechanism used for "Brushing Up," or as complex as the mechanisms used with "The Concert" or "The Moonwalker." The distance between the long axis of the driveshaft and the hole on the crank arm is critical for each particular application. I will refer to this dimension as the "throw" (5) of the crank arm. The peculiar design of the crank arm shown in Fig. 1.07C is necessary if the throw is less than 1/2". This design will prevent the tail of the offset bend on the connecting rod from striking the drive shaft as it rotates.

The drive shaft (1) is made from a 1/4" brass rod with 1/4-20 threads. The brass float arm used in the flush mechanism of a tank toilet is a perfect ready-made substitute. The threaded section of the drive shaft should extend 1-1/2" beyond the nose of the drive shaft mounting block. If the threaded section is shorter than the required 1-1/2", the front side of the hub must be counterbored to accommodate the washer and nut used to secure the propeller to the drive shaft. The crank arm (3) is made from a brass strip .032" thick x 1/4" wide, available in hobby shops that supply materials for model aircraft builders. The crankshaft (4) and connecting rods (6) are formed from 1/16" diameter brass or galvanized wire. The connecting rods are soldered to sleeve bearings (7) made from a 1/8" **I**nside **D**iameter (I.D.) brass tube.

The drive shaft is held in position on the chassis in a drive shaft mounting block. Fig. 1.08 illustrates three variations of drive shaft mounting blocks. The drive shaft extends through the drive shaft mounting block and can be installed with bushings to reduce friction and vibration (B). The front extension of the drive shaft mounting block provides clearance between the propeller and the chassis, as the propeller turns.

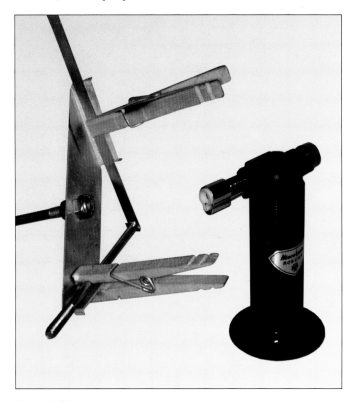

Figure 1.09

The jig, shown in Fig. 1.09, will hold the drive shaft and the crank arm in proper position while soldering or brazing the parts together. The parts are held in the jig with spring activated wooden clothes pins. Do not cut the crank arm to its final length until after it has been soldered or brazed to the drive shaft. Soldering or brazing can be accomplished with a small butane, propane, or acetylene torch.

Connectors (Fig. 1.10 A or B) are attached to the moveable parts of the sculpture at appropriate sites. One of the two styles of connectors illustrated will accommodate any position on the sculpture chosen for

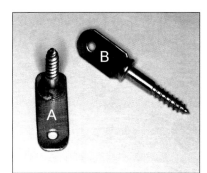

Figure 1.10

installation. The length of the brass strip used for the connector is determined by the particular application for which it is intended. The connectors (Fig. 1.10) are made from #4 x 1/2" solid brass wood screws which have been

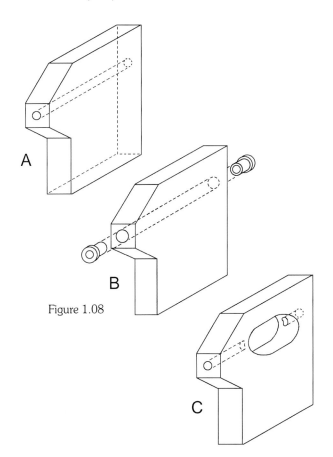

Figure 1.08

7

soldered or brazed to a .032" x 1/4" wide brass strip. The 3/32" hole in the brass strip will accept a 16-gauge brass or galvanized wire connecting rod with an offset bend on the end.

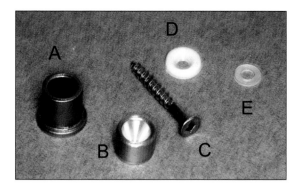

Figure 1.12

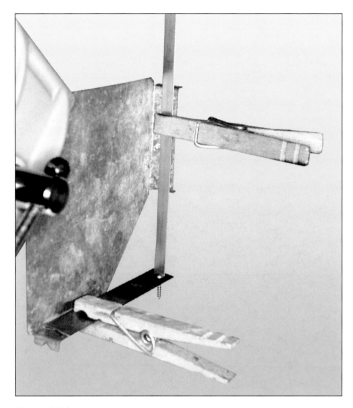

Figure 1.11

The same jig used for the drive shaft/crank arm assembly can also be used to assemble the connectors. An accessory carrier strip will be required to hold the screws in the jig (Fig. 1.11). Do not cut the brass strip to length until after it has been brazed or soldered to the screw. Once the soldering or brazing operation has been completed, the parts can be cleaned and polished with a wire wheel mounted on a bench grinder.

"T," "L," and "I" bars, and brackets are made from .064" half-hard sheet aluminum. This material is available in hobby shops in small pieces (2" x 10") or in large sheets (3' x 4') from industrial suppliers. Full size patterns for the metal parts are glued to the material with spray adhesive and cut out with a bandsaw. The rough edges produced by the saw are eliminated with a file or a bench top belt-sanding machine. The centers for the holes are marked with an awl and drilled or punched with a metal hand punch. The paper pattern is then removed with an adhesive solvent. The sharp metal edges can be rounded and polished with a wire wheel on a bench grinder.

The pivot screws used to attach the "T," "L," and "I" bars to the drive shaft mounting block and to connect the arms and legs to the puppet's body can also benefit from the use of bearings. I recommend the use of nylon countersunk finishing washers under the heads of stainless steel flat head #6 screws and two flat nylon washers on the shank between the moving and stationary parts.

Counterboring the pivot holes in the arms and legs for the finishing washers will greatly improve the appearance of the finished assembly. The size of a nylon washer is designated by the screw size with which it will be used. Bushings (A), bearings (B), a pivot screw (C), and nylon washers (D and E) are pictured in Fig. 1.12. The oil impregnated bronze flanged bushings are available in a wide assortment of sizes and can be mail ordered from industrial suppliers. I have suggested the 1/4" and 5/16" bore sizes for use with the drive shaft mountings blocks, post pivots, and other rotating or sliding parts. Unfortunately I have not been able to locate a source for ready-made bearings for use with the post-pivots. The bearings, however, are easily made with a drill press or metal lathe. All that is required is a brass or stainless steel rod of the appropriate diameter to match the O.D. size of the bushing. The recess at the top of the bearing is formed with a 60° or 90° metal countersink bit, also available from industrial suppliers.

Figure 1.13

Connecting rods are used to link the mechanical parts together and to push, pull, raise or lower the moving parts of the sculpture. The connecting rods are made from 1/16" (16 gauge) soft, galvanized or brass wire formed with offset bends on the ends that fit into the holes in the connectors, and the holes in the mechanical parts. Offset bends create a simple but secure joint between the ends of the connecting rods and the parts into which they are inserted. The offset bends are formed with a needle nose or three-jaw pliers. A special plier, available at hobby shops that cater to model airplane builders, will produce uniform offset bends quickly and efficiently. The length of the rod can be made adjustable if a "Z" bend is formed in the center. Fig. 1.13 shows a model mechanism that employs most of the features just mentioned. This mechanism is used to create the animation of the "Moonwalker" and the "Jogger" and is described in detail in subsequent chapters of this book.

Some useful metal working tools are shown in Fig. 1.14. Pictured are: an offset bending pliers (1), nibbler (2), sheet metal bending tool (3), three prong pliers (4), round nose pliers (5), and a sheet metal hand punch (6). The punch tool comes with seven sets of interchangeable dies and punches to make holes from 3/32" diameter to 9/32" diameter. Fig. 1.15 shows a small brake fastened to a board with a keel that can be held in a bench vise when in use, and removed for storage when it is no longer needed.

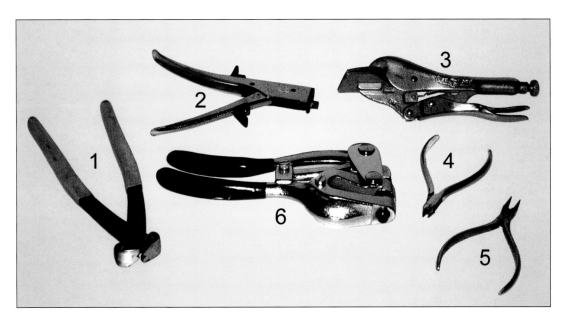

Figure 1.14

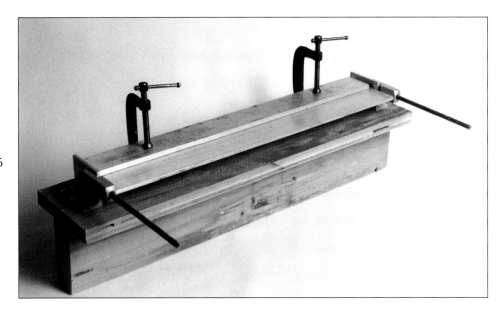

Figure 1.15

Cogwheels

Figure 1.16

The cogwheel is another useful mechanical element for whirligig design and construction. "Planetary Exploration" employs a horizontal cogwheel turned by a sprocket gear. "Time and a Day" is an example of a vertical cogwheel and helical flange gear mechanism. The diameter and number of cogs in the wheel can be varied to meet the physical requirements of their particular application. The cogs are placed at equal intervals around the perimeter of the wheel. I have found a cog interval of about one half inch to be suitable for design and construction purposes. The wooden wheel is cut with a bandsaw and jig that uses the center hole of the wheel as a guide. The cogs are made from brass screws with the heads cut off. Fig. 1.16 shows a three-inch diameter cogwheel with nineteen cogs.

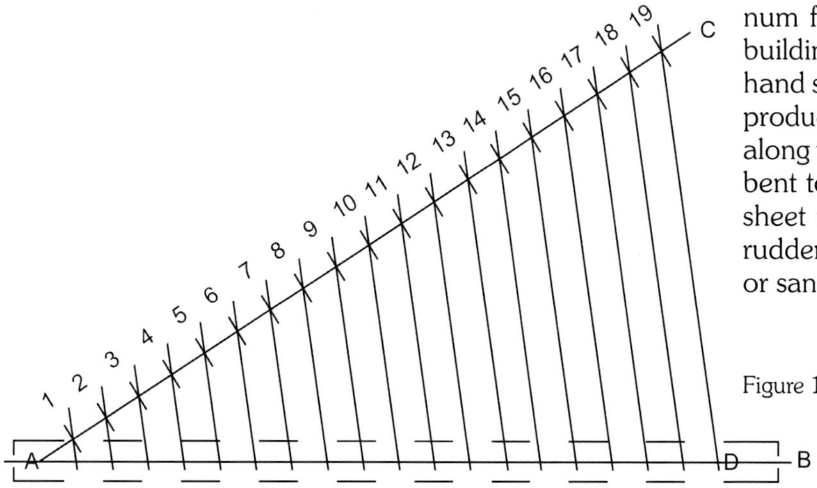

Layout for the position of the cogs must be precise. The following method is recommended to determine the exact position for each cog. This method will work for any diameter wheel with any number of cogs. The diagram in Fig. 1.17 illustrates the steps listed below used to layout the exact cog intervals on a cogwheel with nineteen cogs.

1. On a piece of paper lines AB and AC, which intersect at A, were drawn.
2. Starting at A, 19 points were marked off along AC at half inch intervals. A number from 1 to 19 identified each point.
3. A 1/2-inch wide paper strip of paper was wrapped around the edge of the cogwheel, marked and cut to the exact dimension of the wheel's circumference (AD).
4. The strip of paper was used to transfer dimension AD on to line AB.
5. A line was drawn from 19 to D.
6. Starting at each of the remaining numbered points, lines parallel to 19-D were drawn and extended to intersect AD. These parallel lines divide AD into 19 equal segments.
7. A 3/4-inch strip of paper, indicated by the interrupted lines, which included AD was cut out.
8. The paper strip was wrapped around the edge of the wheel and secured in this position with tape. Points A and D will now coincide.
9. After the position of the cog points was transferred to the edge of the wheel with an awl the paper strip was removed.
10. Using the jig shown in Fig. 1.06 and a drill press, pilot holes were drilled for the cogs.
11. The cogs were chucked into a driver drill and screwed into the pilot holes.

Rudders and Cowls

The rudder can be made from .064" half-hard sheet aluminum. After cutting out the rudder with a bandsaw, the cut edges are filed and polished with a wire wheel. The cowl is made from .025" sheet aluminum or aluminum flashing, which can be purchased in most home building and supply stores. This material can be cut with hand shears. Scoring the material with a sharp knife will produce straight cuts. The material will break if it is bent along the score line several times. The aluminum can be bent to shape in a vise, with a small bench brake or a sheet metal hand tool. The broad, flat surfaces of the rudder and cowl must also be scuffed with a wire wheel or sandpaper in preparation for painting.

Figure 1.17

Post Pivot and Pivot Block

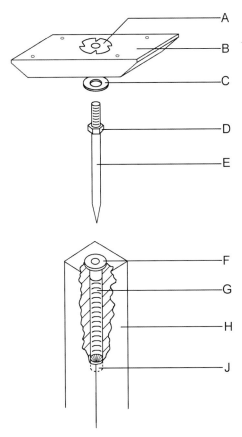

Figure 1.18   "T" nut (A), pivot block (B), washer (C), hex nu t (D), post pivot (E), flanged bushing (F), pivot hole (G), post (H), bearing (J).

Whirligigs must be capable of 360 degrees of rotation in the horizontal plane. To accomplish this, a post pivot on a pivot block is installed under the chassis (Fig. 1.01 B). Fig. 1.18 illustrates the post pivot/pivot block assembly (A-E) and the top end of the post (F, G, H, and J) into which it fits. The post pivot (E) is made from a 5/16-18 x 6" cap screw or carriage bolt with the head cut off. The cut end is pointed for use with a bearing (E) or rounded for use in a hole without a bearing.

After the whirligig has been completely assembled and painted, it is balanced across the edge of a block of wood to locate the center of gravity. The center of gravity is shown marked on a piece of masking tape placed along the edge of the chassis (Fig. 1.19). The pivot block is then installed under the chassis, with the post pivot directly beneath the center of gravity. The pivot fits into a socket formed on the top of the post, as illustrated in Fig. 1.18, or may simply be inserted into a 3/8" hole drilled into the top end of the post.

Figure 1.19

Materials

Because these wind powered machines will be displayed outdoors, they will be exposed to the wind and rain. The construction techniques and materials used for fabrication must be durable and weather resistant. They should be built with hardware made from stainless steel, brass, aluminum or galvanized metal. The projects described in this book use #4, 6, and 8 size screws. Use solid brass or stainless steel (SS) screws with flat head (FH), round head (RH) or oval head configurations as suited for their application. Brass plated steel screws are decorative only and are not recommended because they provide little corrosion resistance. Square drive screws are best, but if they are not available in the sizes needed, Phillips head (PH) screws are a better substitute than slotted screws. Wooden parts should be assembled with exterior or marine adhesives and screws. Assembly can be accomplished with #2, 4, and 6 wood screws of various lengths. Drill pilot holes to guide the path of the screws during installation and to avoid splitting the material. When using soft metal screws (brass and stainless steel) in hard woods the pilot holes should be made slightly larger. Rub beeswax or paraffin into the threads or screws to ease installation. Make clearance holes in the sheet metal parts (rudders, cowls, panels) for the screws used to secure these parts to the wood beneath them. Clearance holes are also required for the moving wooden parts installed with pivot screws.

Slotted brass screws are required to make the connectors described in Fig. 1.10. Use SS or brass bolts, nuts, and washers. Painted surfaces should be protected with several coats of clear gloss varnish. Avoid the use of plywood, which has a tendency to delaminate when exposed to water.

Finishing

A good finish enhances the workmanship of a well-made project. Prepare all wood surfaces by sanding to remove saw marks, knife marks, and other surface imperfections. You will find it helpful to sand and paint many of the parts before assembly. Belt sanders and palm sanders work well on large, flat surfaces. Narrow strips of cloth backed abrasive and abrasive sponges are useful when sanding the irregular contours of the sculptures. Prime or seal coat all the prepared surfaces. When this initial coat dries thoroughly, lightly sand your project again to remove any raised fibers and surface irregularities you may have previously missed.

Fig. 1.20 illustrates some of the supplies and materials that will be useful when decorating your whirligigs. The acrylic paints (5) sold in craft shops are available in an extensive range of colors, in small quantities, at a

reasonable price. The paints are packaged in squeeze containers with a dispensing spout. The paint is opaque, odorless, dries quickly to a flat finish, and is water soluble for easy cleanup. Because the paint is opaque and dries to a flat finish, different colors can be applied over previously painted areas without concern for paint adhesion or bleed through from the underlying colors. A ceramic tile (1), glass slab, or flat dish makes an excellent palette. The paint can be applied with brushes or small sponges. Different sponges will create different textures and markings. Silk sponges (3) will apply the paint evenly with an orange peel texture. Sea sponges (4) will create a mottled effect, which is excellent for blending different shades of color. Elephant ear sponges (2) are useful to apply paint in corners and can be used to produce narrow strips of color. Do not overload the sponge when applying paint. Load the sponge from paint on a palette. Dab the sponge on a clean area of the palette until it is almost dry, to remove excess paint. Apply the paint to the surface with a light, tamping motion until you create the effect you desire. Masking tape (6) and stencils (7) can be used to paint areas with a clean, sharp edge. The adhesive on masking tape often tears off the paint beneath it during removal. To avoid this problem, reduce the adhesive properties of the tape by applying it to fabric (i.e. your clothing) and removing it several times before applying it to your project. A razor blade (8) is useful to remove the dried paint from the ceramic palette.

When the paint has dried thoroughly, apply several coats of clear gloss acrylic varnish or spray with a clear

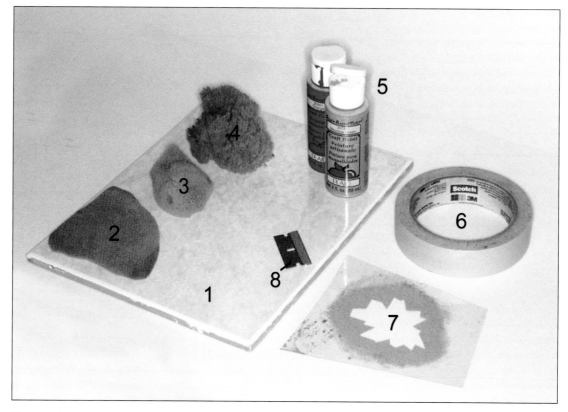

Figure 1.20

gloss media. The clear gloss finish intensifies the colors beneath it and creates an attractive, lustrous, weatherproof surface. Airbrushes may also be used to apply paint. Acrylic paint, unfortunately, tends to clog in the nozzle of an airbrush because it dries so quickly. It becomes excessively time consuming to clean the airbrush to clear the nozzle of dried paint and when changing colors. Aerosol cans of spray paints are more suitable, but they are available in a limited range of colors. I have found the aerosol cans of clear gloss to be the most practical method for applying the final surface finish on my whirligigs projects. Apply the spray in several light coats to avoid drip marks.

The base and adjustable column of a woodwork support stand can be modified by replacing the roller with a 20" round platform (Fig. 1.21), to create a convenient support for painting and spraying your whirligig. Two of these tables with "V" blocks, placed several feet apart, are useful for supporting the post for your whirligig stand while painting, decorating, and spraying this part. Properly constructed and finished, your whirligig will provide years of amusement, and require minimal maintenance and repairs.

Patterns, Plans, Illustrations, and Instructions

All the patterns, plans, and illustrations shown have been prepared to scale and will be labeled full size (FS), half size (FS/2) or quarter size (FS/4). Some detailed drawings of the larger parts have been reduced in size to fit the available space and dimensions have been provided as required. Features hidden from view in illustrations will be shown as interrupted lines or grayed out. Footprints are used to indicate the location of objects that have been omitted from the drawings for clarity. Bending lines are shown as interrupted lines and have been labeled accordingly. Symbols used in the illustrations to indicate the size and locations of holes to be prepared prior to assembly are identified on each drawing.

FS/2 patterns will have to be enlarged to FS for use. The easiest and most accurate way to enlarge FS/2 patterns to FS is to have them reproduced at 200% at your neighborhood copy center. If your computer is equipped with a scanner, printer, and image editing program, it is possible to enlarge FS/2 patterns by scanning them at 200% or scanning them at 100%, and doubling the photo size. The resulting FS image can be printed out as a FS pattern. If the image is larger than the paper

your printer can accept, the FS image can be printed as overlapping sections and assembled with clear tape. If you chose to enlarge or reduce the patterns to a size other than the full size recommended you will have to make adjustments for the size of the hardware and thickness of the materials.

Paper patterns can be secured directly to the material to be cut with spray adhesive. This is most helpful when cutting, drilling and punching metal parts. The paper patterns can then be removed by saturating them with an adhesive solvent.

Some patterns are shown with views of adjacent surfaces. These patterns are to be folded over the edge of the material to which they will be applied and indicate layout information on more than one surface.

The parts used for each project are designated by letters and can be identified using the Parts and Materials List that accompanies each project. The instructions in the book contain abbreviations for commonly used fasteners. Screws have been designated as round head (RH), flat head (FH), and/or stainless steel (SS).

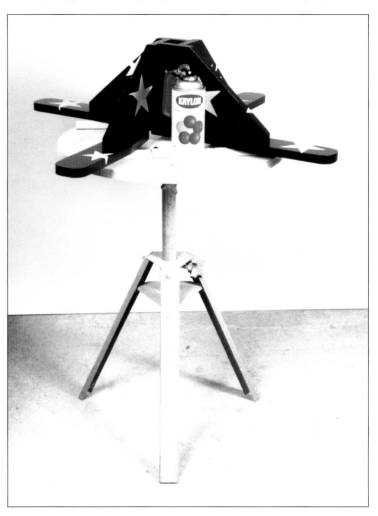

Figure 1.21

13

Stand Construction

The whirligigs described in this book are not built to operate above 100 RPM. To prevent them from becoming damaged, they should not be exposed to wind conditions that will cause them to exceed this limit. The portable stand suggested in this book can be made with a second, short post for indoor storage and tabletop display of the whirligig during periods of high wind and inclement weather.

Figure 1.23

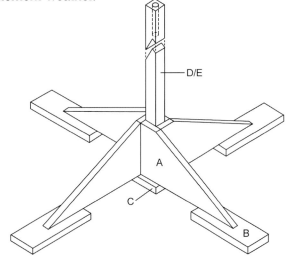

Figure 1.22

Whirligigs should be displayed slightly above eye level, where they can be conveniently viewed and will operate efficiently. The portable stand illustrated in Fig. 1.22 will allow the whirligig to be moved as required for display and wind conditions. The post, which fits loosely into a socket at the center of the base, is removable to facilitate transportation and storage. The post is secured in the socket with two thumbscrews fitted into "T" nuts on two adjacent sides of the socket (Fig. 1.23).

The stand may be stabilized by placing heavy objects over the feet or by anchoring the feet to the ground with stakes. Concrete blocks, which fit over the feet, can be cast as shown in Fig. 1.23. Each block measures 4" W x 3-1/2" H x 9" L. One bag of premixed concrete will make eight weights. Four of these blocks are used for each stand, to provide ballast of about thirty-two pounds, which will prevent the stand from blowing over on a windy day.

The base of the stand is constructed from a 3/4" thick pine board. The cutting diagram shown in Fig. 1.24 provides the most efficient use of the material. Lay out and cut the parts as shown. Drill a large hole in the center of the socket base (C) for drainage of any rainwater that might accumulate when your whirligig is displayed outdoors. A long and short post (D/E) can be made from a piece of cedar 1-1/2" x 1-1/2" x 96" of ripped from and 2 x 3 or 2 x 4. The extra short post is useful to support your whirligig at a convenient working height during assembly, painting, and adjustment procedures.

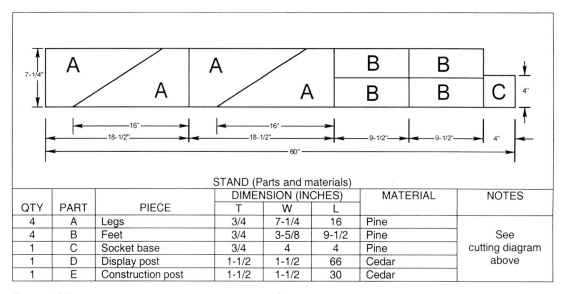

STAND (Parts and materials)

QTY	PART	PIECE	DIMENSION (INCHES)			MATERIAL	NOTES
			T	W	L		
4	A	Legs	3/4	7-1/4	16	Pine	
4	B	Feet	3/4	3-5/8	9-1/2	Pine	See cutting diagram above
1	C	Socket base	3/4	4	4	Pine	
1	D	Display post	1-1/2	1-1/2	66	Cedar	
1	E	Construction post	1-1/2	1-1/2	30	Cedar	

Figure 1.24

Chapter 2

Brushing Up

This whirligig is an *excellent* first project. It requires basic wood-working, metalworking, and painting skills. The entire project can easily be completed in one weekend. The mechanical system is simple, easily assembled, and adjusted. My whirligig is conspicuously displayed near the entrance to my dental office to remind my young patients to "brush up." I'm not sure how effective this display has been, but it has attracted a great deal of attention. Fig. 2.01 is a photograph of the completed work.

Fig. 2.02 and the parts and materials list (Fig. 2.03) will iden-

Figure 2.01

tify the labeled parts in all subsequent illustrations. Begin by making parts A-H using the patterns provided in Figs. 2.04-05. Part F will be made as a pair. Designate and label one of the pair as F (left) and the other F (right). The complex joint formed when A, B, D, and G are assembled will require nine screws. The location of the counterbored pilot holes for these screws is shown on the patterns for these parts. Screws placed at these locations will not interfere with one another or the addition of the post pivot, which will be added at a later stage of construction.

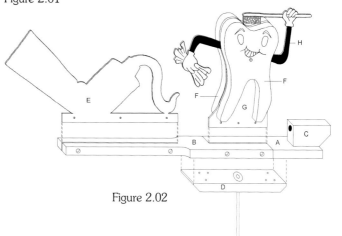

Figure 2.02

Figure 2.03

BRUSHING UP (Parts and materials)							
QTY	PART	PIECE	DIMENSION (INCHES)			MATERIAL	NOTES
			T	W	L		
1	A	Chassis front section	3/4	1-5/8	9-1/4	Poplar or pine	FS/2 Pattern
1	B	Chassis back section	3/4	1-5/8	17-3/4	Poplar or pine	FS/2 Pattern
1	C	Drive shaft mtg. block	3/4	1-3/4	3-1/4	Poplar or pine	FS/2Pattern
1	D	Post pivot mtg. block	3/4	1/5/8	8	Poplar or pine	FS/2 Pattern
1	E	Rudder	.064			Aluminum	FS/2 Pattern
2	F	Tooth L&R sides	3/4	5-5/8	9	Poplar or pine	FS/2 Pattern
1	G	Tooth center section	1/8	5	4-3/4	Poplar or pine	FS/2 Pattern
1	H	Tooth arms and eyes	.064	12	15-1/4	Aluminum	FS/2 Pattern
1	J	Pivot for H	#6 x 1-1/4" screw			Brass	Cut off screw head
1	K	Drive shaft/crank arm	7/32"	End threaded rod		Brass	See Section 1
1	L	Propeller assembly	2 or 3 blades			See Chapter 2	Propeller assembly
1	M	Post and stand				See Section 1 Figs. 1.27-1.29	

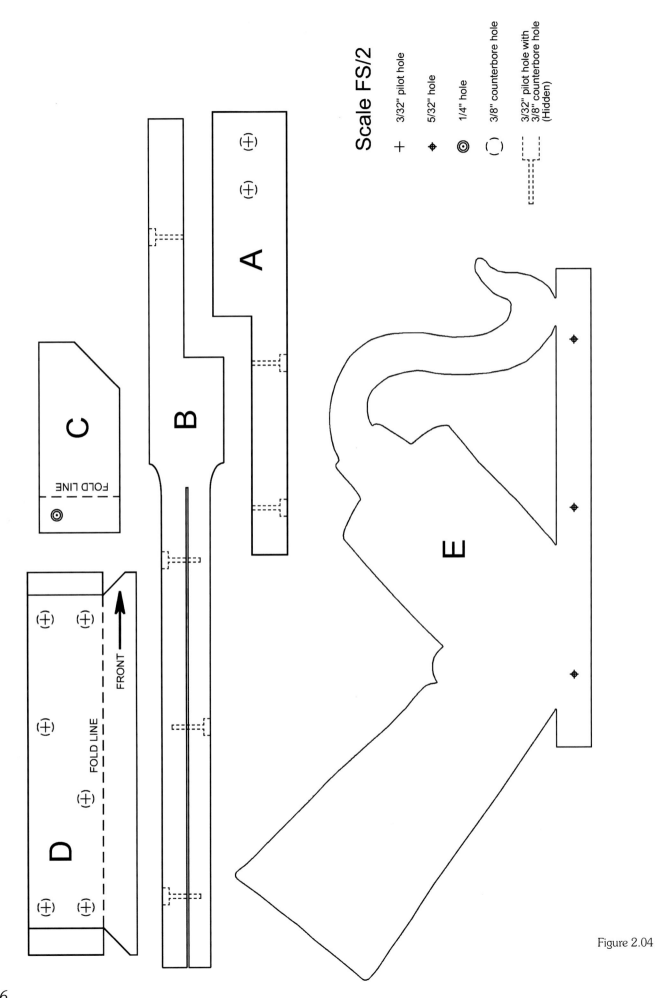

Scale FS/2

+ 3/32" pilot hole

◆ 5/32" hole

◎ 1/4" hole

⬡ 3/8" counterbore hole

3/32" pilot hole with
3/8" counterbore hole
(Hidden)

A

B

C
FOLD LINE

D
FOLD LINE
FRONT

E

Figure 2.04

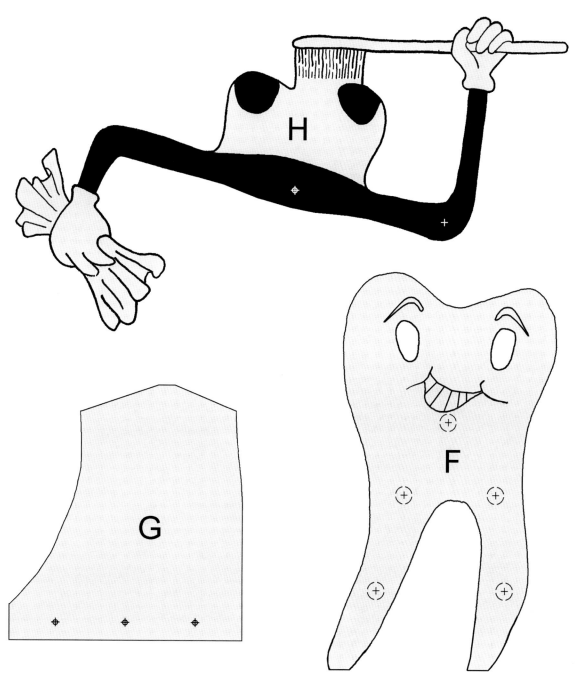

Scale FS/2

+   3/32" hole

⊕   5/32" hole

◯   3/8" counterbored hole

Figure 2.05

Drill and counterbore four assembly holes for the screws that will be used to join F and G. Drill and counterbore a fifth assembly hole for the pivot screw (J). Drill these holes on only F (right). The position of these holes is shown on the pattern for F. These holes will be plugged after final assembly. Make a trial assemble of F (left) and F (right) with G using four #6 x 1-1/4" SS screws (Fig. 2.06).

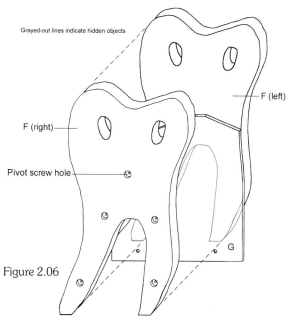

Grayed-out lines indicate hidden objects

F (left)

F (right)

Pivot screw hole

G

Figure 2.06

Carve and sand the contours as suggested in Fig. 2.07. Disassemble F and G to paint, decorate, and varnish these parts. Be sure to paint and varnish the inner surfaces of the slot in the tooth's upper body for H.

Cut out and punch or drill the holes in H as shown in the pattern for this part. Paint, decorate, and varnish both sides as shown. Assemble F, G, and H using #6 x 1-1/4" SS FH screws. Fill the assembly holes with face grain plugs. Touch up the plugged holes with paint and varnish to conceal these areas.

The chassis is formed by the assembly of A, B, and D with six #6 x 1-1/4" SS screws, as shown in Fig. 2.02. Position D so that it is centered under the slot between A and B. Fasten C to the chassis assembly with two #6 x 1-1/4" SS screws. Paint and varnish the assembly as suggested in Fig. 2.01.

quired (Fig. 2.08). Construct a propeller with three 1/4" x 3-1/2" x 8" blades. After painting and varnishing, install the propeller on the threaded front end of the drive shaft. See Chapter 1 for details of this procedure. Cut out the rudder from a piece of .064 sheet aluminum using a full size enlargement of the pattern shown in Fig. 2.04. Paint and varnish the rudder before installing it in the slot in B with three #6 x 3/4" SS screws. Install the completed tooth assembly (F-G-F and H) as shown in Fig. 2.02 with three #6 x 1-1/4" SS screws.

Balance the completed assembly over the edge of a board and locate the center of balance on D. Remove D from the assembly to install a post pivot at the center of balance as described in Chapter 1. Reconnect D to the chassis to complete the whirligig.

All you need now is a stand in a breezy location to watch your little tooth scrub himself clean

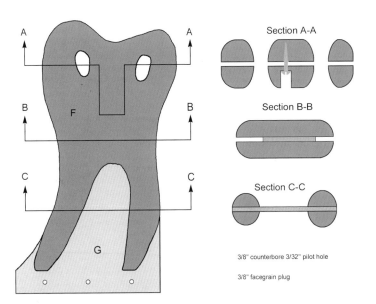

Figure 2.07

Fabricate a drive shaft and crank arm with a 1/2" throw as described in Chapter 1 and shown in Fig. 1.07. Install the drive shaft/crank arm in the drive shaft mounting block with a few brass or SS washers on either end to reduce friction. Bend a connecting rod from a 12-inch piece of 1/16" diameter (16 gauge) brass or galvanized wire with an adjustment bent in the middle. Install the rod between the crank arm and H and adjust as re-

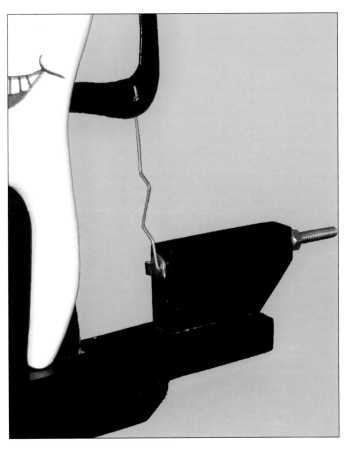

Figure 2.08

Chapter 3

Superstar

Today's star performers usually attract thousands of fans to a single concert. This whirligig represents one of these performances. Fig. 3.01 is a photograph of the completed project with the star playing his guitar before the footlights of the stage. Superstar is an ideal project for the bandsaw enthusiast.

This whirligig is composed of the following assemblies: (1) stand, (2) propeller, drive mechanism, and mechanical linkage, (3) chassis assembly, and (4) puppet. Details for the construction of (1) and (2) can be found in Chapter 1 of this book. Construction of the puppet and chassis assembly will be described here. The cutting list (Fig. 3.02) will identify the parts shown in Figs. 3.03 – 3.05. Enlarge the FS/2 patterns to full size and secure them to the material listed for their fabrication. Cut out parts A-E, G, and H. The patterns for F and K are shown FS and indicate layout positions on adjacent surfaces of the material. These patterns must be folded along the indicated lines and secured to the material on two surfaces.

The puppet assembly consists of parts A-F. The left arm (F) must be compound cut on the bandsaw from a block of wood 1-1/2" x 2" x 7". The block can be made by gluing two 3/4" x 2" x 7" pieces of wood together. Secure the pattern to the side and top of the block with spray adhesive. Make the cuts shown by the interrupted lines first. Tack the waste material back on the block. Turn the block so that the outline of the arm is facing upward and complete the cutting operation.

Figure 3.01

Figure 3.02

SUPERSTAR (Parts and materials)						
			DIMENSION (INCHES)			
QTY	PART	NAME	T	W	L	MATERIAL	NOTES
1	A	Left leg and torso	1/2	3-1/2	12	Poplar or pine	FS Pattern
1	B	Head and center torso	1/2	3	9	Poplar or pine	FS Pattern
1	C	Right leg, torso, guitar	1/2	5	10	Poplar or pine	FS Pattern
1	D	Guitar handle	1/2	1	6-1/2	Poplar or pine	FS Pattern
1	E	Right arm	1/2	4	5	Poplar or pine	FS Pattern
1	F	Left arm	1-1/2	2	7	Poplar or pine	FS Pattern
1	G	Platform	3/4	3-1/2	3-1/2	Poplar or pine	FS/2 Pattern
1	H	Rudder	.064	12	24	Aluminum	FS/2 Pattern
1	J	Chassis	3/4	1	30	Poplar or pine	
1	K	Drive shaft mtg. block	3/4			Poplar or pine	FS Pattern
1	L	Propeller assembly	2 blades 1/4 x 3-1/2 x 12				Fig. 1.02
1	M	Post pivot assembly				See Section 1	Fig. 1.18
1	N	Stand					Fig. 1.23-1.25

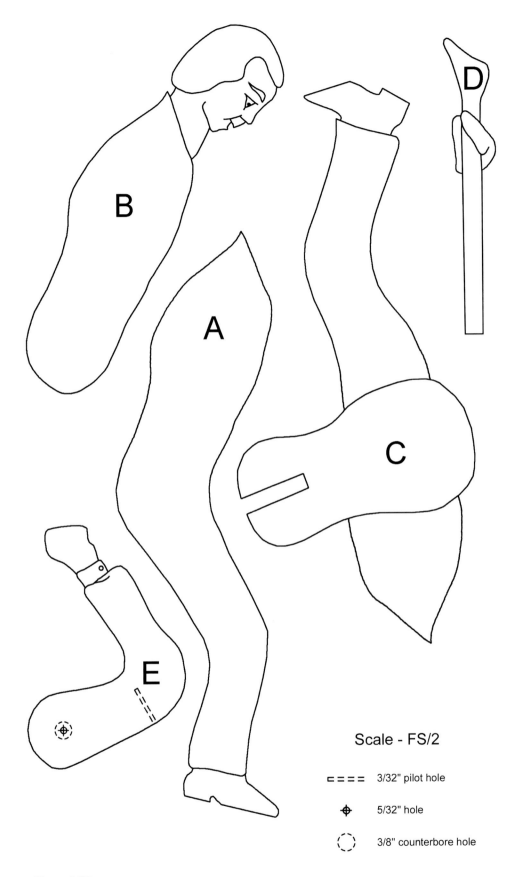

Scale - FS/2

⊏ ⊏ ⊏ ⊏ 3/32" pilot hole

⊕ 5/32" hole

3/8" counterbore hole

Figure 3.03

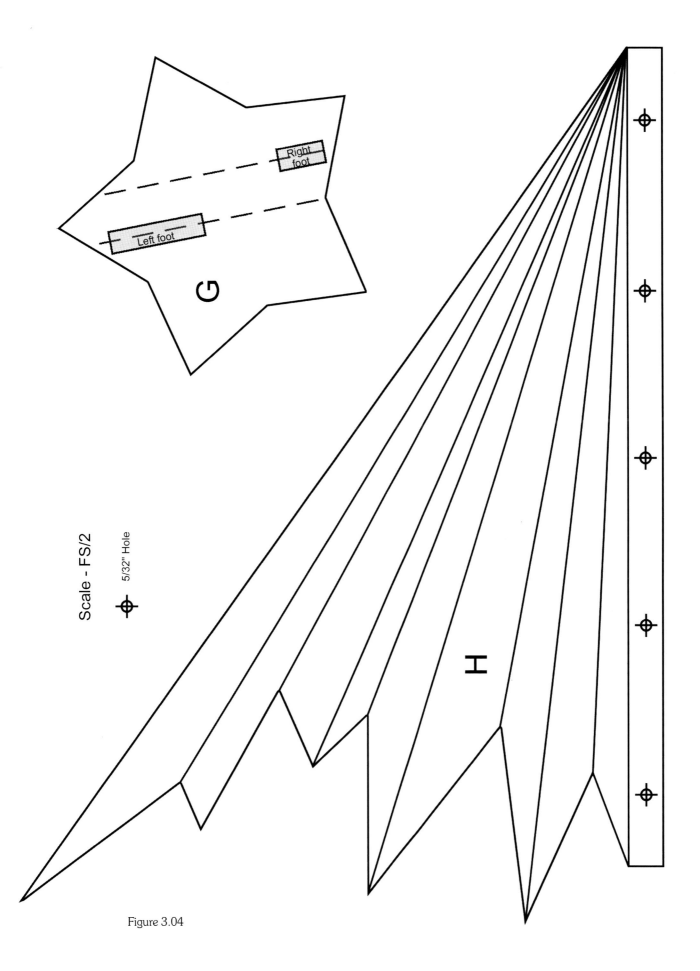

G

Right
foot

Left foot

Scale - FS/2

⊕ 5/32" Hole

H

Figure 3.04

21

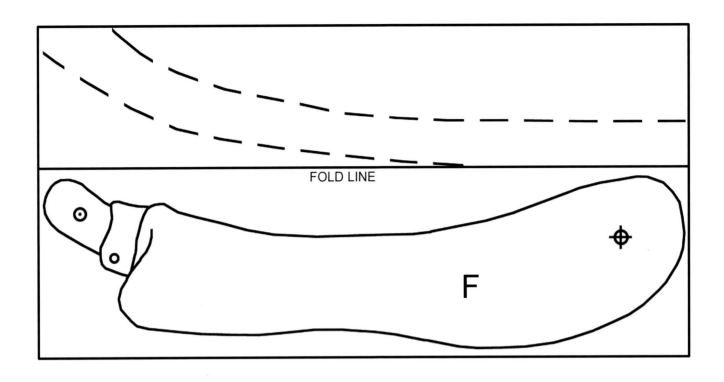

FOLD LINE

F

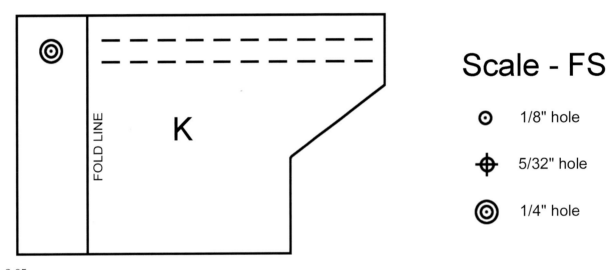

FOLD LINE

K

Scale - FS

⊙   1/8" hole

⊕   5/32" hole

◎   1/4" hole

Figure 3.05

Assemble parts A-D with waterproof glue and screws. Carve and sand the puppet's body and arms to suit before continuing assembly. The puppet's right arm pivots on a #6 x 1-1/4" RH wood screw at the shoulder. Use one washer under the screw head and two washers between the arm and the body to prevent friction between the moving parts. Install a connector (Fig. 3.06) in the pilot hold of the puppet's right arm (E) as shown on the FS pattern (Fig. 3.03). Screw the shoulder of the left arm (F) to the puppet's body and the wrist to the hand on the guitar with a small screw. Fasten the completely assembled puppet to the platform (G) with two # 6 x 1-1/2" screws from below the platform (G). The pattern for G indicates the position of the puppet's feet on top by the gray rectangles and the position of the chassis beneath by the interrupted lines.

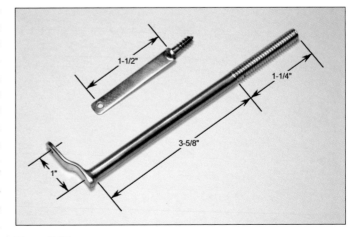

Figure 3.06

Cut a 1/16" wide slot in the back end of the chassis (J) for the rudder (H). Secure the rudder in the slot with screws in counterbored pilot holes. Fasten the drive shaft mounting block to the front end of the chassis (J) with two #6 x 1-1/2" screws. Insert a drive shaft, with a crank arm that has a 1" throw, in the drive shaft mounting block. Install the puppet, platform assembly on the chassis behind the drive shaft mounting block so that the end of the arm's connector is directly above the crank arm of the drive shaft. Connect the crank arm to the connector on the puppet's right arm with an adjustable wire connecting rod. Adjust the length of the connecting rod to create the desired arm position and motion. Fig. 3.07 illustrates this mechanical linkage. Install a propeller with two 3-1/2" x 12" blades (Fig. 1.02) on the front end of the drive shaft.

Partially disassemble the whirligig to simplify painting and finishing and reassembled when the painting has been completed. Install a post pivot and pivot block as described in Chapter 1.

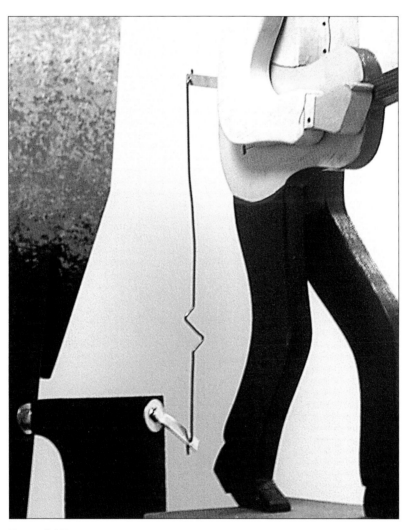

Figure 3.07

Chapter 4

Violin Concerto

The concerto is a musical composition that features a solo musician with orchestral accompaniment. The music is arranged to emphasize the soloist's extraordinary skill and talent. For the audience, the concerto is the most important and highly anticipated segment of the concert program. This whirligig represents a violin concerto performance. Fig. 4.01 is a photograph of the completed whirligig. The Parts and Materials list (Fig. 4.02) will identify the labeled items in the illustrations that follow.

Figure 4.01

Figure 4.02

VIOLIN CONCERTO (Parts and materials)							
QTY	PART	PIECE	DIMENSION (INCHES)			SUGGESTED MATERIAL	NOTES
			T	W	L		
1	A	Chassis	3/4	1-1/4	26-1/2	Poplar/Pine	Fig.VC.03
1	B	Drive shaft mtg. block	3/4	3-1/2	5-3/8	Maple/Oak	Fig. 1.08
1	C	Rudder	.064	18-1/2	12-1/2	Aluminum	FS/4 pattern
1	D	Platform	3/4	4-1/2	5-3/4	Poplar/Pine	Oval shape
1	E	Torso/left leg	1/2	5-1/2	11-3/4	Poplar	FS/2 pattern
1	F	Torso center section	1/2	2-1/2	8-1/2	Poplar	FS/2 pattern
1	G	Torso/right leg	1/2	3-1/2	11-3/4	Poplar	FS/2 pattern
1	H	Left arm	1/2	3-1/2	6	Poplar	FS pattern
1	J	Right arm	1/2	1-3/8	4-1/2	Poplar	FS pattern
1	K	Shoulder/violin	1/2	5-1/2	8-1/2	Poplar	FS pattern
1	L	Head	3/4	2-1/4	2-1/2	Poplar	FS pattern
1	M	Violin bow	1/8 diameter		3	Dowel	
1	N	Drive shaft/crank arm	1/4 diameter		5-1/4	Brass	Fig. VC.10
1	P	"L" bar	.064	1-7/16	5-1/8	Aluminum	FS pattern
1	Q	Long arm connector	.032	1/4	2	Brass	Fig. VC.10
1	R	Connecting rod	16 gauge wire			Galv/brass	Fig. VC.10
1	S	Connecting rod	16 gauge wire			Galv/brass	Fig. VC.10
1	T	Right arm hinge pin	16 gauge wire			Galv/brass	Fig. VC.10
1	U	Propeller assembly	2 blades ¼ x 3-1/2 x 12			See Section 1	Fig. 1.02
1	V	Post pivot assembly					Fig. 1.18
1	W	Post and stand					Fig. 1.23-1.25

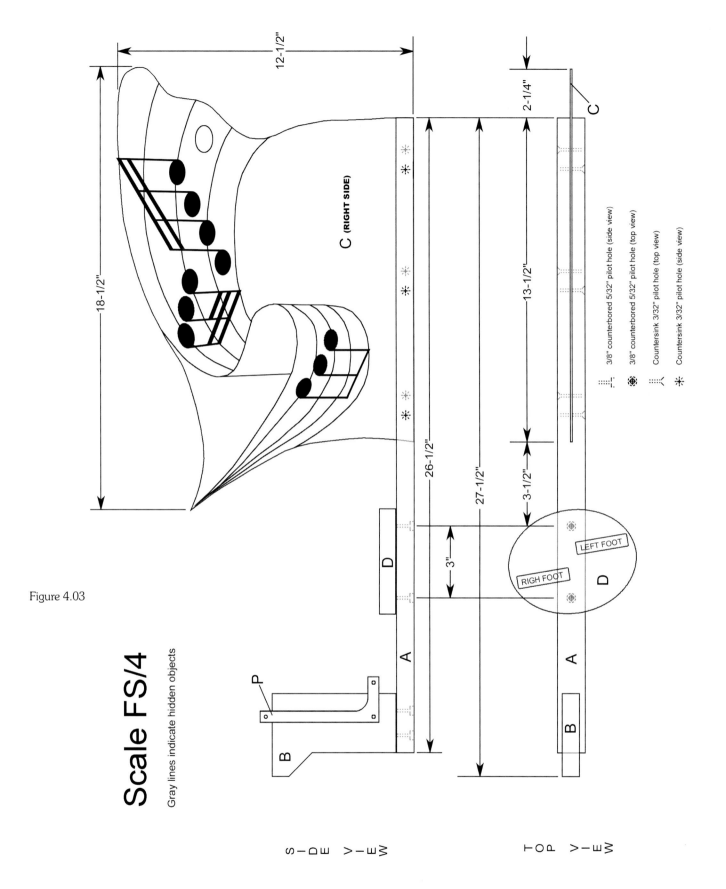

Figure 4.03

Scale FS/4

Gray lines indicate hidden objects

Fig.4.03 illustrates the chassis assembly. Make the driveshaft-mounting block (B) using a FS enlargement of its pattern (Fig. 4.04). Bore a slightly oversized hole for the drive shaft to minimize friction and allow it to rotate freely in the block. Better still, use 1/4" ID flanged bushings and bore the hole to accommodate the outside dimension of the fitting (Fig.1.08B). Make a 3/32" pilot hole for the pivot screw for P, as shown on the pattern. Attach B to A with two #6 x 1-1/4" FH screws.

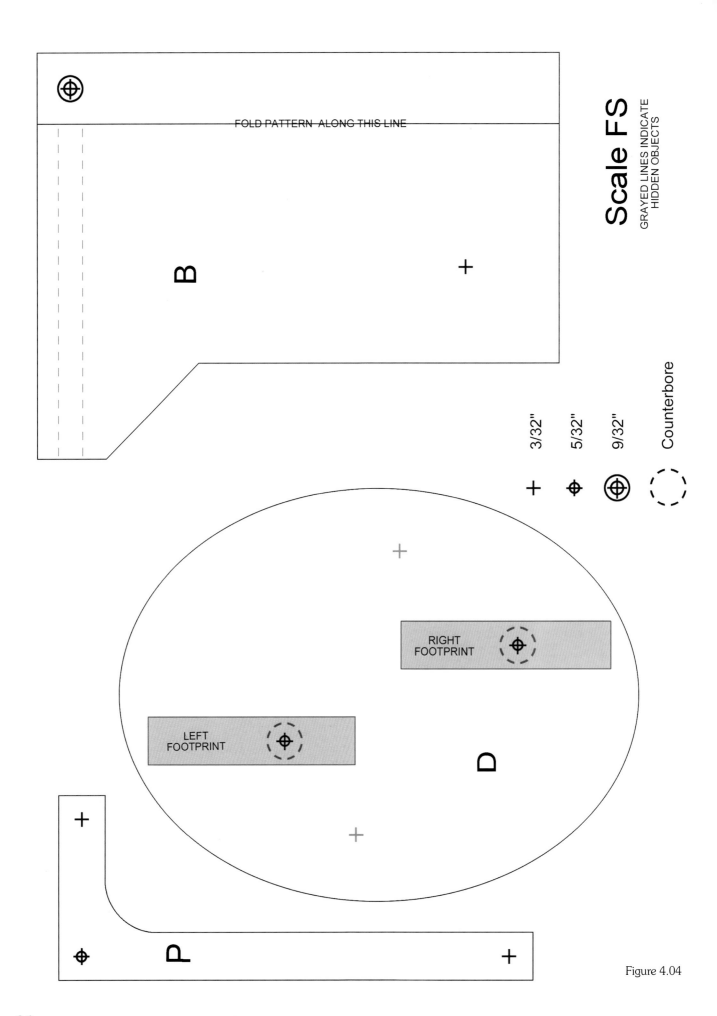

FOLD PATTERN ALONG THIS LINE

Scale FS

GRAYED LINES INDICATE
HIDDEN OBJECTS

B

Counterbore

3/32"   +

5/32"   ⊕

9/32"   ⊕

RIGHT
FOOTPRINT

LEFT
FOOTPRINT

D

P

Figure 4.04

26

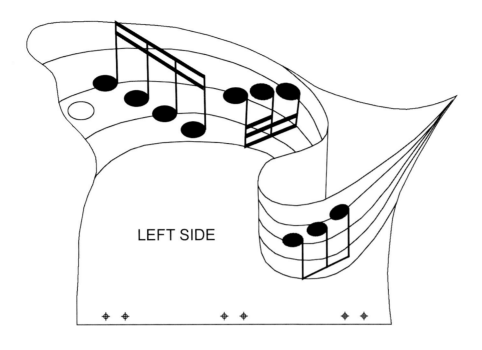

LEFT SIDE

Scale FS/4

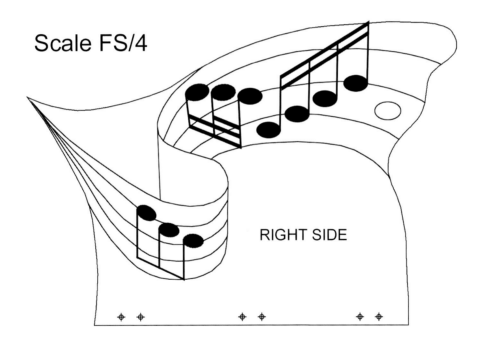

RIGHT SIDE

Figure 4.05

Cut out the rudder (C) from a piece of .064 half hard aluminum using a FS enlargement of the pattern in Fig. 4.05 and drill or punch the six mounting holes along the bottom edge. The design for the left and right side of the rudder have been provided because they are slightly different. Paint the rudder as shown in the design for the right and left sides. The rudder will be installed after the chassis assembly has been painted. Use the rudder as a template to layout the position of the 3/32" pilot holes in

A. Layout, drill, and countersink the pilot holes from alternate sides of the slotted end of the chassis (A) as shown in Fig. 4.03. Assemble and paint the chassis/driveshaft-mounting block assembly. Install P on B with a #6 x 1" pivot screw in the previously prepared pilot hole. Use several washers under P so that it will not contact B during operation. Install the rudder in the slot in A and secure it with #6 x 1" FH screws in the holes prepared for this purpose.

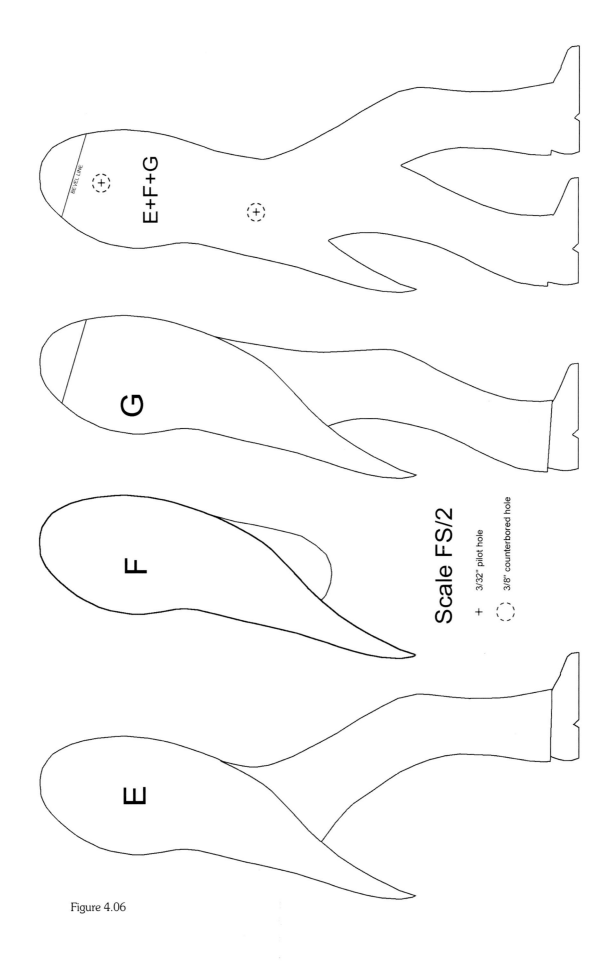

E+F+G

BEVEL LINE

G

F

E

Scale FS/2

+   3/32" pilot hole

(+)   3/8" counterbored hole

Figure 4.06

28

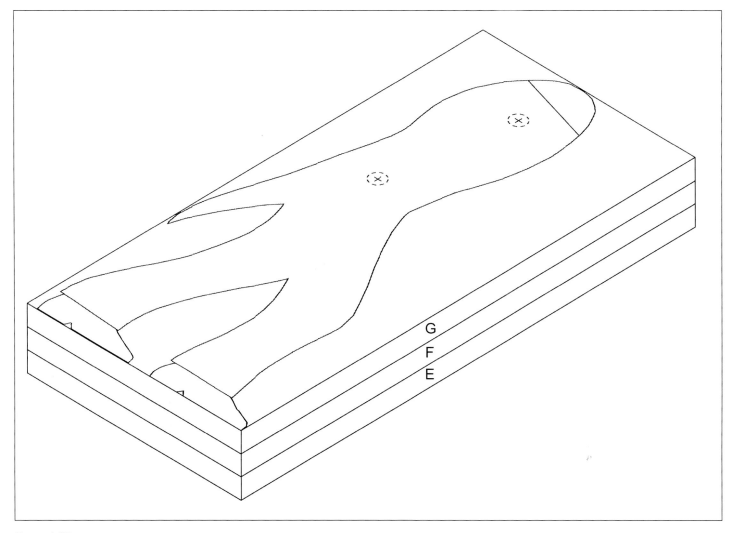

Figure 4.07

The violinist's body is built from parts E, F, G, H, J, K, and L. The body and legs (E+F+G) are gang cut from a block made from three pieces of poplar 1/2" x 5-1/2" x 11-3/4" joined with two #6 x 1-1/4" screws (Fig. 4.06 and 4.07). Gang-cut the assembled block to the profile of the combined shape of E, F, and G with a bandsaw or scroll saw. Bevel the top of the torso from the bevel line to the top outside edge of the left shoulder. K will be secured to this flat surface at a subsequent stage of construction. Disassemble the block and save the screws for reassembly. Transfer the individual patterns of E, F, and G (Fig. 4.06) to the appropriate sections and cut off the unwanted parts. This technique will produce an assembly that will fit together accurately when reassembled. Carve and sand the parts to round off and shape the torso, legs, and shoes. Counterbore the screw holes in G for 3/8" face grain plugs and reassemble E, F, and G with glue and screws. Cut 1/4" off the point of the screws before reusing to prevent them from protruding through the opposite side of the body. Use face grain plugs to conceal the heads of the screws.

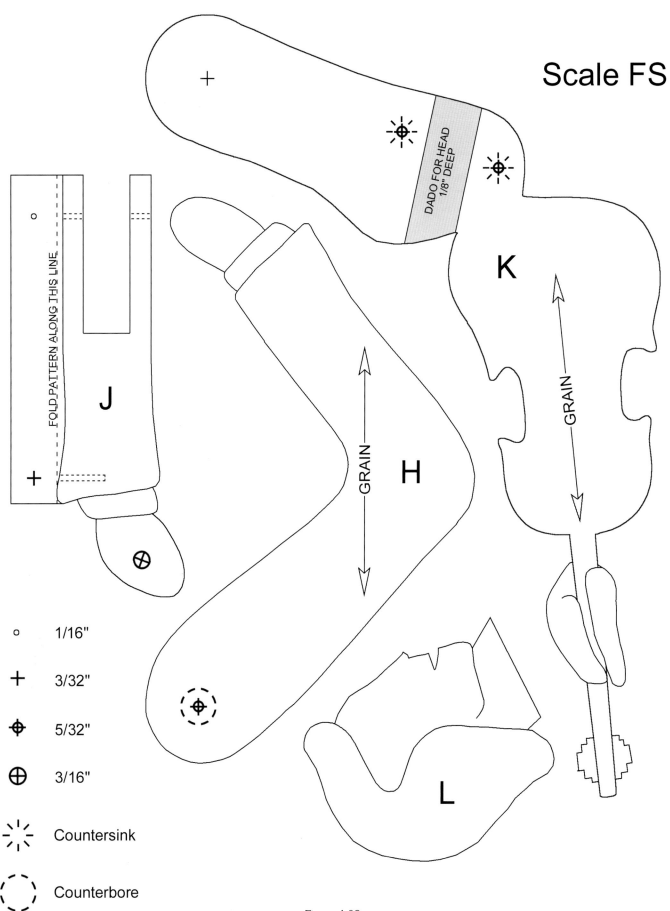

Scale FS

DADO FOR HEAD
1/8" DEEP

FOLD PATTERN ALONG THIS LINE

J

K

GRAIN

GRAIN

H

L

○   1/16"

+   3/32"

⊕   5/32"

⊕   3/16"

Countersink

Counterbore

Figure 4.08

Cut out parts H, J, K, and L (Fig. 4.08). Drill the holes and cut the dado as indicated on the patterns. Temporarily attach H to the left shoulder of the torso assembly with a #6 x 1-1/4" wood screw. Align K on the beveled surface of the body assembly so that the wrist of H is beneath the violinist's left hand on the neck of the violin. Temporarily secure K in this position with two #6 x 1-1/4" FH wood screws. Bevel the wrist on H to fit against the back of the hand on K.

Carve K to conform to the upper torso and narrow the neck of the violin to develop the puppet's hand. Carve H to round off the arm and shape the left wrist. Carve L in low relief to shape the head. Remove K from its position on the torso and fasten L in the dado with glue and screws. Carve J to round off the square edges and form the cuff and right hand.

Drill a 3/16" blind hole in the palm of the right hand for the violin bow (M). Install the long arm connector into the pilot hole under the violinist's right wrist. Fit the slotted end of J over the right shoulder of K. Use T to pin the arm (J) in place and allow it to swing freely. Make adjustments as required. Install a 3/16" x 5" dowel (M) in the right hand of J to represent the violin bow. These details are shown in Fig. 4.09A/B).

Secure the puppet to the platform (D) using two #6 x 1-1/4" FH screws from beneath the platform into the puppet's legs. Countersink the 5/32" clearance holes to recess the heads of the screws. Remove J and D from the puppet assembly to paint the parts. Fig. 4.10 shows the violinist when viewed from the right, front, and left sides.

The puppet/platform assembly is oriented on the chassis in a skewed position. To accomplish this task correctly, the mounting holes on A and D must be accurately located and drilled. See Fig. 4.03 for the details required to lay out and drill the 3/8"counterbored x 5/32" clearance holes in A. The 3/32" pilot holes in D are indicated on the FS pattern for this part (Fig. 4.04). Position D above the chassis with the pilot holes

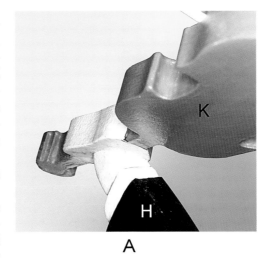

A

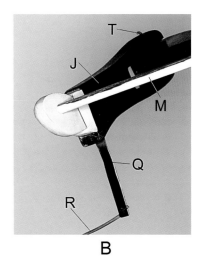

B

Figure 4.09

Figure 4.10

directly above the mounting holes in A. Use two #6 x 1-1/4" screws to join D to A. Reassemble the puppet on the platform (D). It will now be oriented at the correct angle with the driveshaft-mounting block (B). Reassemble J on K with T. Bend over the protruding lower end of T to prevent it from becoming dislodged.

Fig. 4.11 provides the dimensions required for fabricating parts Q, N, R, and S. Fig.4.12 illustrates the mechanical drive train that produces the animation for the puppet violinist. Install connecting rods R and S as shown in the photograph. Test the mechanism and make adjustments as required by opening or closing the "Z" bends in the center of each rod.

Make a propeller with two 1/4" x 3-1/2" x 12" blades. After balancing and paintings the propeller, it must be installed so that the center of gravity of the completed whirligig can be determined. Install a post pivot directly beneath the center of gravity. Complete the whirligig by making a stand and post to support and display your whirligig in a breezy location.

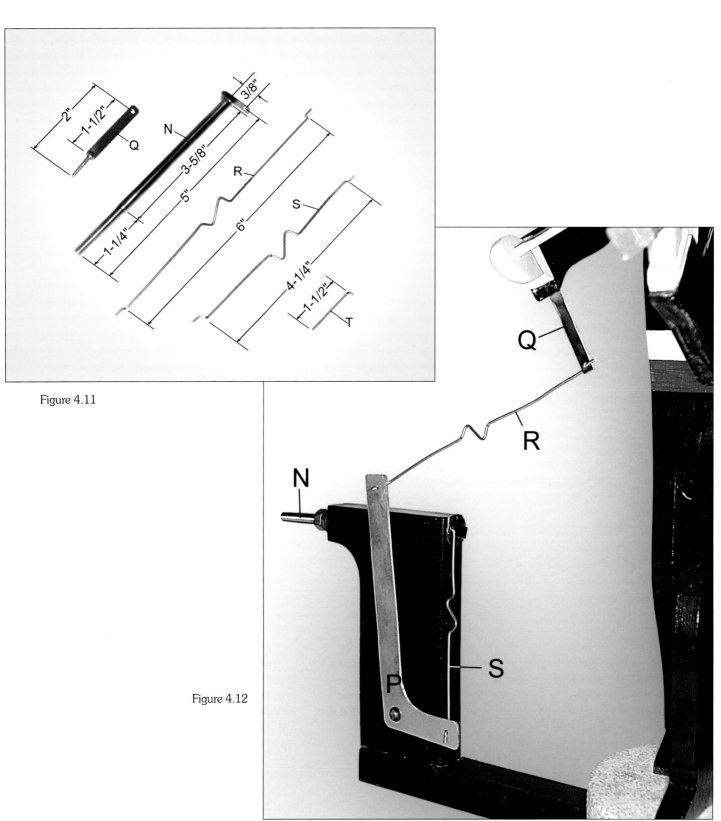

Figure 4.11

Figure 4.12

Chapter 5

The Cyclist

Bicycling has become a popular pastime for recreation and exercise. My home is at an intersection where several local cycling clubs pass every weekend. Watching these cyclists speeding by inspired this whirligig, which can keep up with the best of them with a light breeze. It was displayed outside my home for several years, until the pedal crank finally wore out. The Cyclist is now resting on my workbench, awaiting repairs needed for next season's cycling activities. Fig. 5.01 is a photograph of the completed project.

Construction of this whirligig requires some precision woodworking operations and some basic metal working techniques. The mechanical components of the drive train are simple. The challenging work for this project is the construction of the puppet's hip and knee joints. These joints must operate smoothly, without binding or rubbing. Allowance must be made for the paint that will be applied to the surfaces inside the joints and for expansion of the wood during periods of rain and high humidity. The parts and materials list (Fig. 5.02) and Fig. 5.03 will identify the labeled parts in all the illustrations that follow.

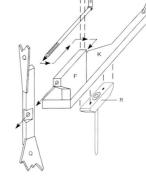

Figure
5.03

Figure 5.01

Figure 5.02

CYCLIST (Parts and Materials)							
QTY	PART	NAME	DIMENSION (INCHES)			MATERIAL	NOTES
			T	W	L		
1	A	Center body section	3/4	2-3/4	9	Poplar or pine	
2	B	Outer body section	5/8	2-3/4	9	Poplar or pine	
2	C	Arms	5/8	2	5-1/2	Poplar or pine	
2	D	Thighs	5/8	1-3/4	4-3/4	Poplar or pine	
2	E	Legs	5/8	2-2/4	4	Poplar or pine	FS/2 patterns
1	F	Drive shaft mtg block	3/4	3	3-1/4	Poplar or pine	
2	G	Wheel	.064	6	6	Aluminum	
1	H	Bicycle frame	5/8	6-1/2	11	Poplar or pine	
1	J	Rudder	.064	6-1/2	15	Aluminum	
1	K	Chassis	3/4	2-5/8	15	Poplar or pine	
1	L	Pedal crank bracket	.064	1-5/8	2-1/2	Aluminum	Fig. C.08
1	M	Puppet support post	3/8 Diam.		9	Poplar or pine	
1	N	Handle bar	1/4" Diam.		4	Dowel	
3	O	Hip/knee joint pivots	3/16" Diam.			Dowel	
1	P	Pedal crank arm	16 Gauge		5	Brass/galv. wire	
2	Q	Propeller blades	1/4	3-1/2	12	Part 1 Fig. 1.02 and related text	
1	R	Post pivot assembly				Part 1 Fig. 1.18 and related text	
1	S	Stand				Part 1 Figs. 1.22. 1.23 and 1.24	

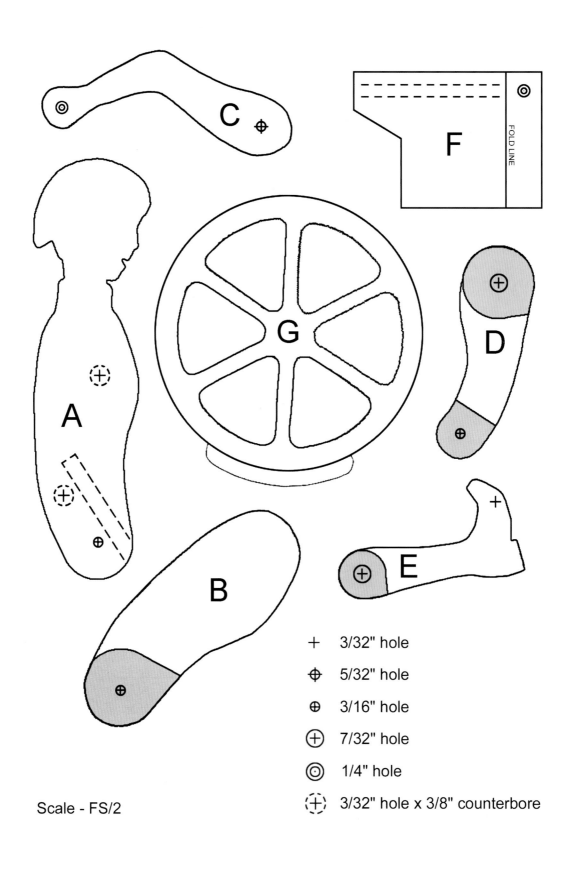

C

F FOLD LINE

A

G

D

B

E

+   3/32" hole

⊕   5/32" hole

⊕   3/16" hole

⊕   7/32" hole

◎   1/4" hole

⊕   3/32" hole x 3/8" counterbore

Scale - FS/2

Before starting construction, enlarge the half size patterns in Fig. 5.04 and Fig. 5.05 to full size.

Figure 5.04

34

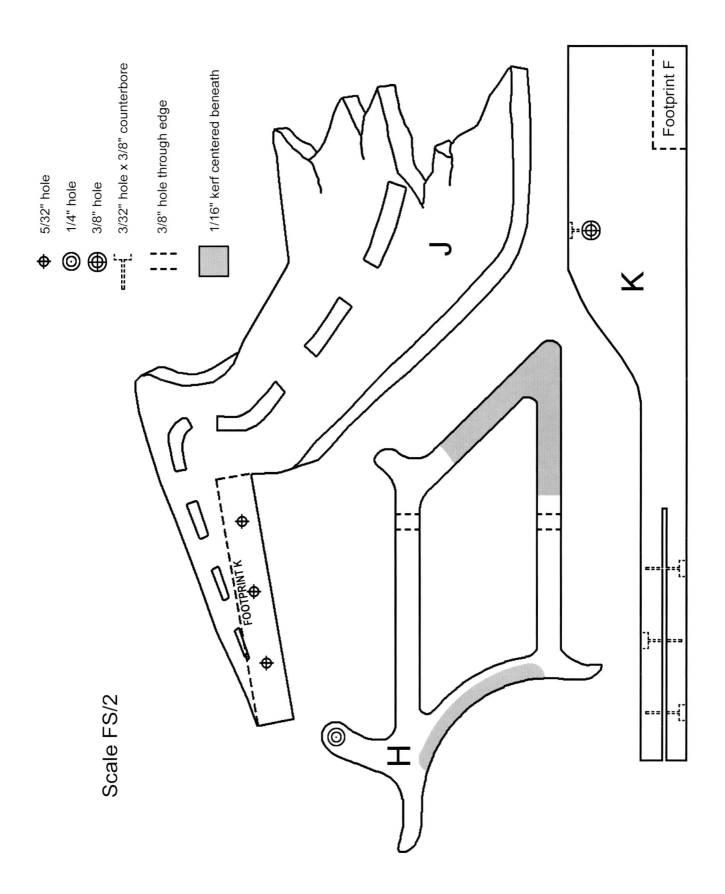

Scale FS/2

5/32" hole

1/4" hole

3/8" hole

3/32" hole x 3/8" counterbore

3/8" hole through edge

1/16" kerf centered beneath

Footprint F

FOOTPRINT K

J

K

H

Figure 5.05

Make the puppet's body by stacking blocks of wood B-A-B and layout A on the stacked blocks (Fig. 5.06). Drill and counterbore holes for two #6 x 1-1/2" FH wood screws used to connect the layers during construction. These holes will be plugged after final assembly to conceal the screws. Gang cut the assembled blocks to the shape of the center body section (A). Use a drill press to make a 3/16" hole for the hip joint pin. Remove the center body section from the stack and reassemble the block. Cut off the head and neck from the remaining two pieces of the block, as shown on the pattern of B, to complete the form of the outer body sections. Drill a 3/8" hole up into the center body section (A) for the support post (M). I used a dowel jig to accurately drill this hole.

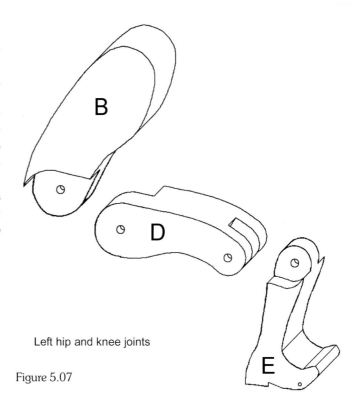

Left hip and knee joints

Figure 5.07

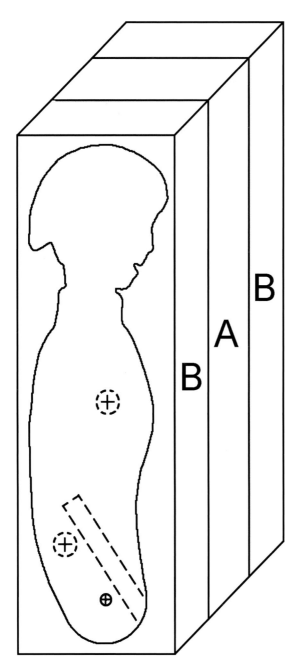

Figure 5.06

Gang cut parts C, D, and E to make the cyclist's arms and legs. The arms and legs will be made as a pair, one right and one left. The drilling and milling operations that follow must be accomplished with this in mind. Drill 5/32" holes in the arms (C) for #6 screws and 1/4" holes through the hands for the handle bar. Drill a 7/32" hole in D for the hip joint pin and 3/16" holes for the knee joint pins. Make 3/32" holes through the feet for the pedal crank arm. The location of these holes is shown on the patterns for these parts. Details of the hip joint and knee joint are shown in Fig. 5.07. The lower end of B and the upper end of D form the half lap rotating hip joints. Form the 3/8" deep recess into B and D as indicated by the shaded areas of the patterns for these parts. Most of the recess can be formed with a 1-5/8" Forstner bit in a drill press. The remaining material for the recess can be removed with a chisel or knife. A 1/4" tongue on E and a 5/16" slot in D forms the knee joint. The shape of the tongue and the slot are indicated on the patterns for D and E as shaded areas. Most of the tongue can be formed with a 1-1/8" Forstner bit to reduce both sides of E until a 1/4" tongue remains. Use a knife or chisel to remove the remaining material to complete the tongue. The 5/16" slot can be made with a bandsaw. Carve and sand the body, arms, and legs to remove the square edges and contour the body parts.

Dry assemble the puppet's body and legs to test the joints. Use 3/16" dowels for the hip and knee joint pivots (O). The hip and knee joints should swing freely without rubbing or binding. Make adjustments as required. Once the joints are operating properly, the puppet's body can be glued and screwed together. Conceal the screw heads with wood plugs.

Cut out the bicycle frame (H) from a 5/8" thick block of wood. Make slots in the frame for the wheels (G) with a slot cutting router bit. The location of the slots is indicated on the pattern of L as shaded areas. Drill a 1/4" hole for the handle bar and a 3/8" hole for the puppet support post (M). Cut out the wheels (G). Only the front wheel has the extension shown on the pattern. Install the wheels in the slots, and secure them in position with small brass screws. Use the puppet support post (M) to connect the puppet's body to the bicycle. The handle bar, made from a 1/4" x 4" dowel, is added to the bicycle and held in position with a small screw. Slide the hands of C on each side of the handle bar. Adjust the position of the arms until the shoulders are in correct position against the puppet's body. Use #6 screws through the shoulders to connect the arms (C) to the body.

K, F, and J comprise the chassis assembly. Cut a 1/16" wide slot in the end of the chassis (K) for the rudder (J). Drill a 3/8" hole in the chassis for the sculpture support post (M). Drill and counterbore holes in the edges of K for screws to secure the rudder (J) and mounting post (M) to the chassis (K).

Fig. 5.08 illustrates the dimensions and assembly of the mechanical parts used with this whirligig. The pedal crank arm (P) must be added to the pedal crank bracket before it is installed on the bicycle frame. Fig. 5.09 provides the dimensions and a FS pattern for the bracket (L). The notch at the end of H fits against M to accurately position the pedal crank bracket under the bicycle frame (H). The ends of the crank arm wires pass through the puppet's feet. The longer end of the crank arm goes through the cyclist's right foot.

Mount the puppet and bicycle on the chassis and adjust the height of the bicycle until the rotational axis of the pedal crank is in line with the axis of the drive shaft. Use a #6 screw through the edge of K into M to secure the puppet assembly in this position. Cut off the protruding end of the mounting post flush with the bottom of the chassis.

Use a two-blade propeller (Q) to activate this whirligig. Install a post pivot under the chassis and make a stand to support the completed whirligig. Details and instructions for these parts are provided in Chapter 1.

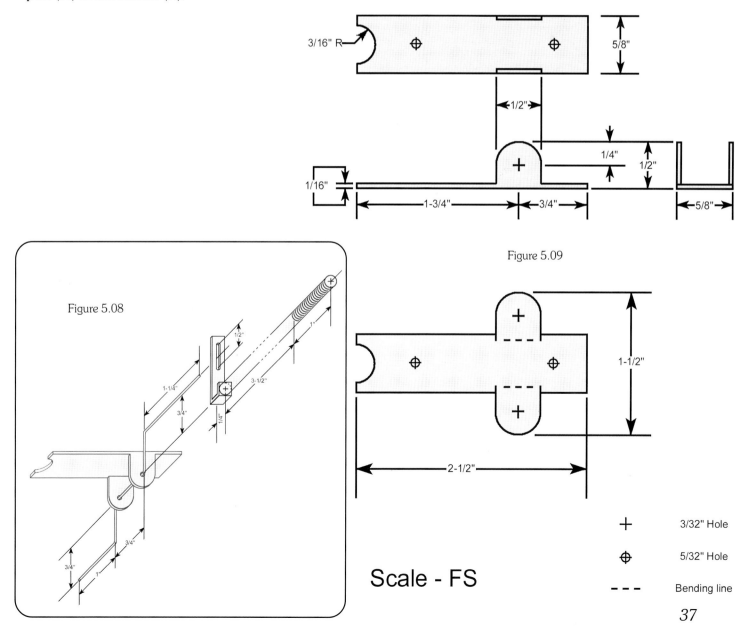

Figure 5.09

Figure 5.08

Scale - FS

+	3/32" Hole
⊕	5/32" Hole
- - -	Bending line

Chapter 6
Moonwalker

On July 20, 1969, the U.S. astronaut Neil Armstrong landed his lunar module and stepped out to become the first man on the moon. "The Moonwalker" (Fig. 6.01) represents this remarkable event in the history of space exploration. The unique feature of the whirligig is the drive train mechanism, which produces the coordinated arm and leg movements of the puppet astronaut as he walks across the moon to place the U.S. flag upon its surface.

Figure 6.01

		MOONWALKER PARTS AND MATERIALS				
			DIMENSION (INCHES)			
QTY	PART	PIECE	T	W	L	SUGGESTED MATERIAL
1	A	Chassis	3/4	2-1/2	28	Poplar/Pine
1	B	Drive shaft mtg block	3/4	3-1/4	6	Maple/Oak
1	C	Upper cowl support	3/4	2-1/2	3	Poplar/Pine
2	D	Standoff blocks (L&R)	1/2	1	2	Poplar/Pine
1	E	Rudder	.064	11	13-5/8	Aluminum
1	F	Cowl	.025	9	14	Aluminum
1	G	Post pivot block	3/4	2-1/2	4	Poplar/Pine
1	H	Puppet support post	3/8 Diam.		10	Dowel
1	J	Puppet body	2-1/2	2-3/4	9	Poplar
2	K	Puppet legs (L&R)	1	2-1/2	5-3/4	Poplar
1	L	Puppet right arm	3/4	3	5-1/4	Poplar
1	M	Puppet left arm	3/4	3	5-3/4	Poplar
1	N	Puppet back pack	3/4	2-1/8	3-3/8	Poplar
1	O	Reciprocating bar	.064	1/2	2	Aluminum
2	P	Arm/leg activating bar	.064	1-3/8	4-7/8	Aluminum
1	Q	Flag pole	1/8	1/8	4	Brass rod
1	R	Flag	.025	1-1/2	2-1/2	Brass/Copper

Figure 6.02

Fig. 6.02 lists and identifies the labeled parts in all the subsequent illustrations. Details for fabrication of the propeller, specialty hardware, stand, and post pivot have been provided in Chapter 1, and will not be repeated. Please refer back to the appropriate pages for information required to make these items. I recommend a propeller with four 3-1/2" x 12" blades for this whirligig.

Fig. 6.03 illustrates the chassis assembly, which should be completed as the initial stage of construction for this whirligig. Cut out the chassis (A), drill all holes, and make a 1/16" wide slot for the rudder and drill all holes as shown in Fig. 6.04. The remaining parts are shown in Fig. 6.05-07 or described in Fig. 6.02. Glue the standoff blocks (D) on both sides of B and drill pilot hole for the pivot screws that will be used to mount O and P to the assembly. The location of the 3/32" pilot holes is indicted on the FS patterns for B.

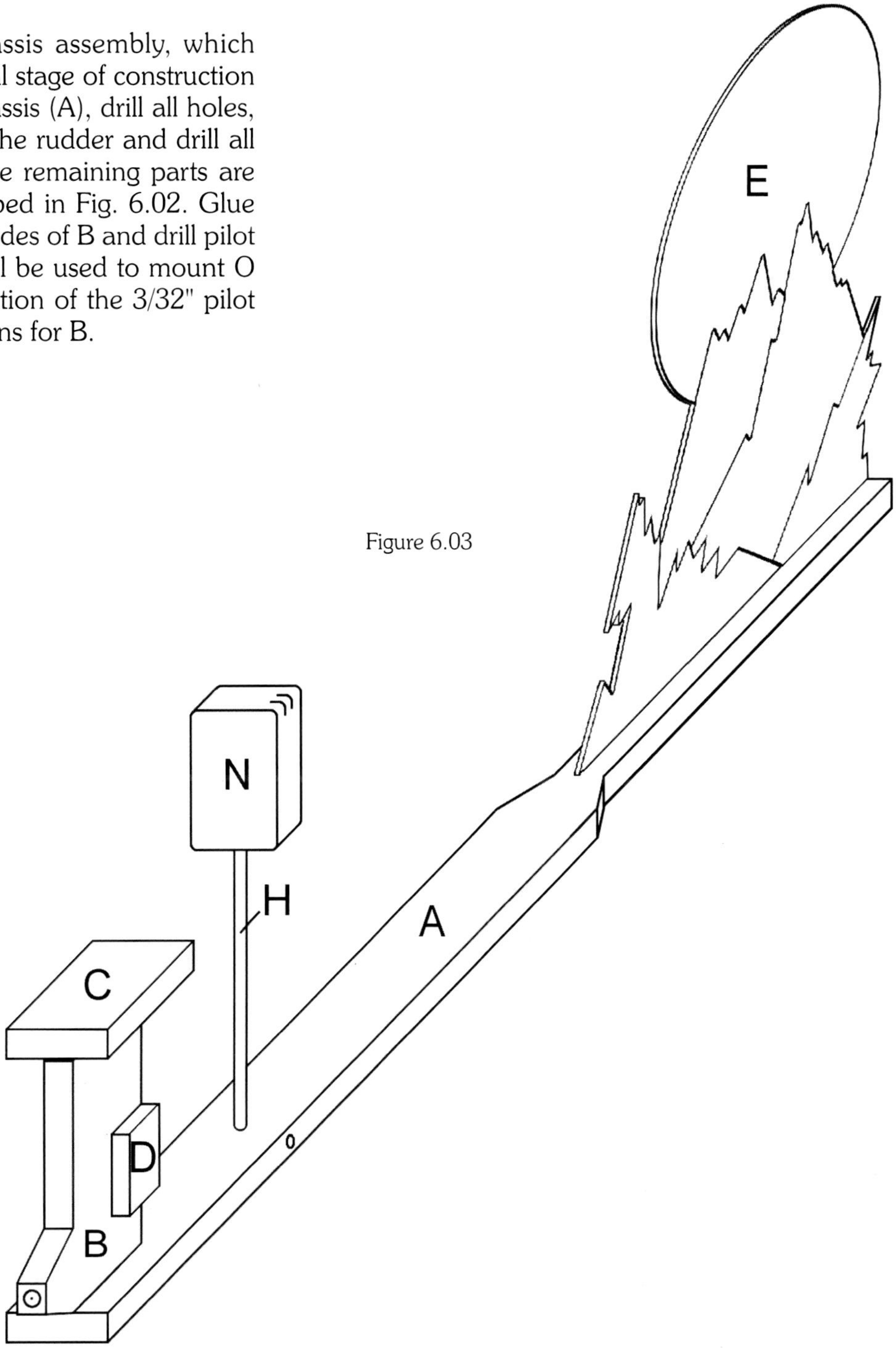
E
N
H
A
C
D
B

Figure 6.03

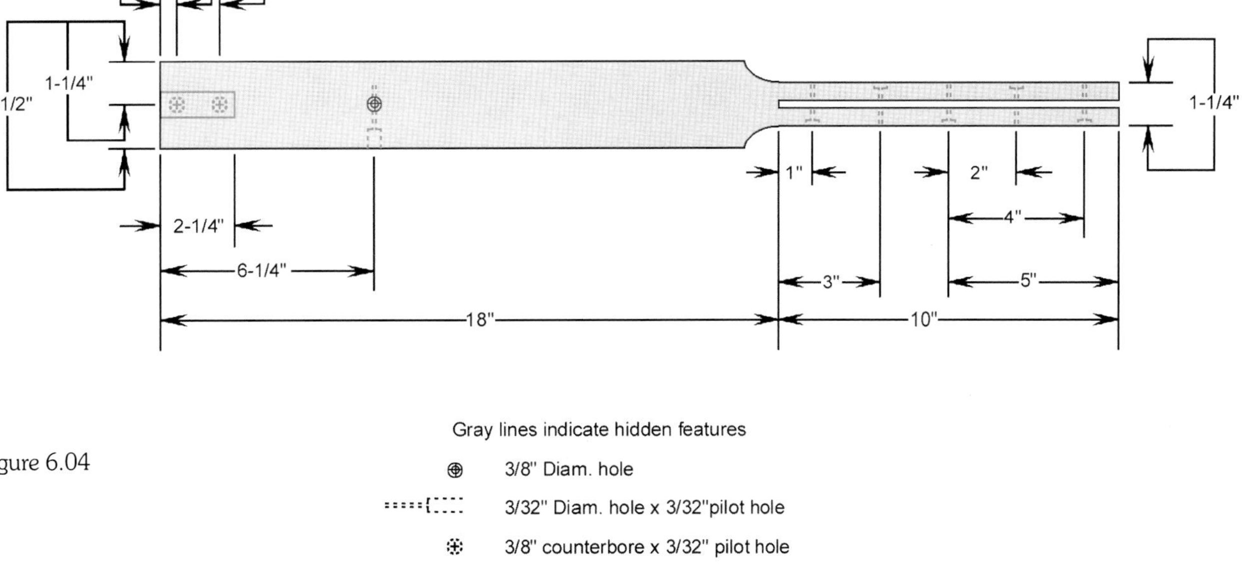
1-11/16"
9/16"
2-1/2"
1-1/4"
1-1/4"
1"
2"
4"
2-1/4"
6-1/4"
3"
5"
18"
10"
Gray lines indicate hidden features
3/8" Diam. hole
3/32" Diam. hole x 3/32"pilot hole
3/8" counterbore x 3/32" pilot hole

Figure 6.04

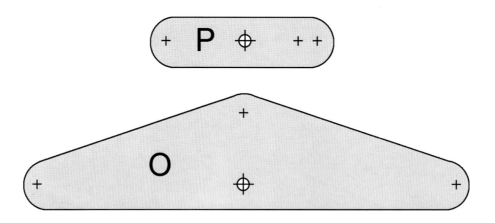

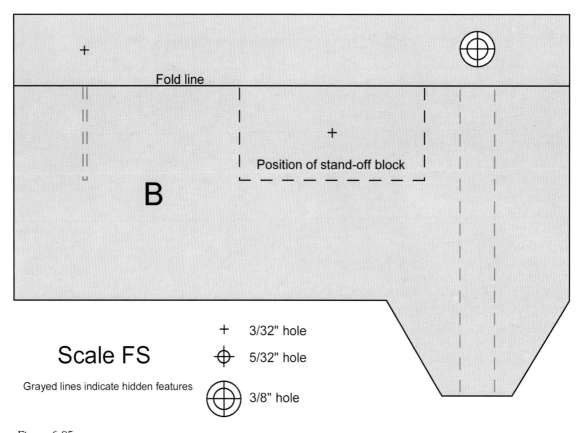

Fold line

Position of stand-off block

B

Scale FS

Grayed lines indicate hidden features

+   3/32" hole

⊕   5/32" hole

⊕   3/8" hole

Figure 6.05

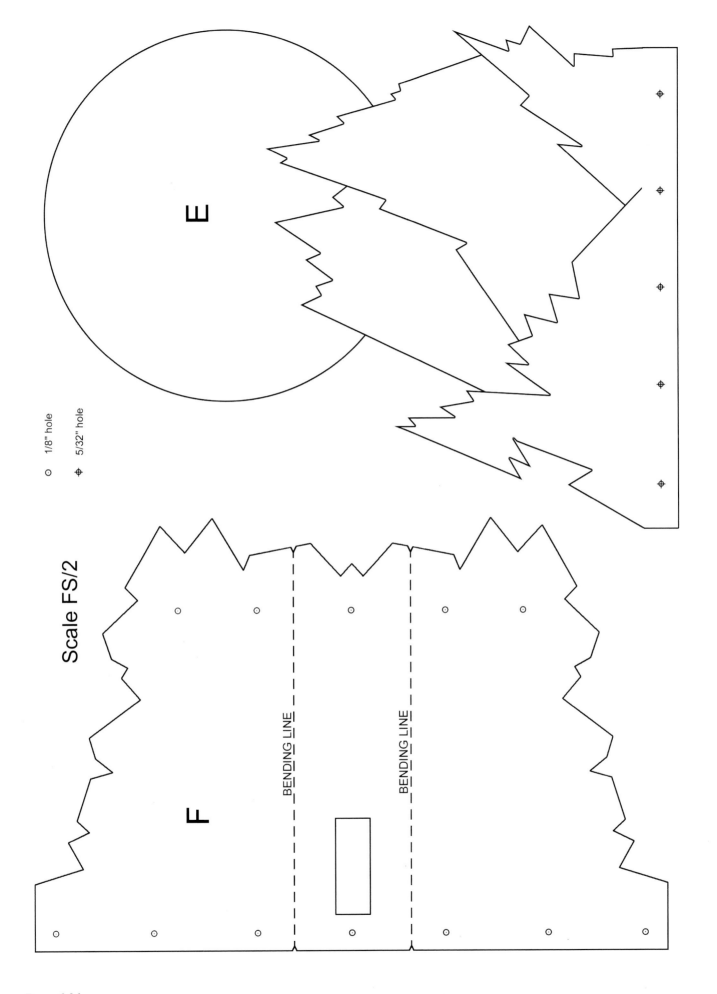

Scale FS/2

○ 1/8" hole

⊕ 5/32" hole

E

F

BENDING LINE

BENDING LINE

Figure 6.06

41

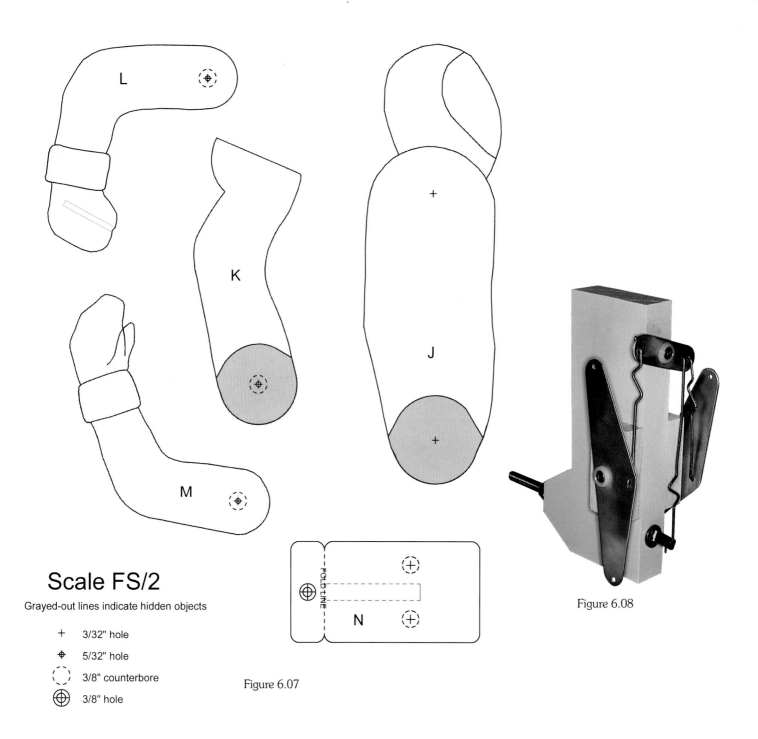

L

K

M

J

Scale FS/2

Grayed-out lines indicate hidden objects

+	3/32" hole
⊕	5/32" hole
⊙	3/8" counterbore
⊕	3/8" hole

FOLD LINE

N

Figure 6.07

Figure 6.08

Once the chassis assembly has been completed the mechanical drive may be installed as shown in Fig.6.08. Install flanged bushings in the front and rear ends of the 3/8" hole for the drive shaft. The front end of the driveshaft should be threaded for 1-1/2" and extend beyond the nose of the driveshaft mounting block (B) this distance. The crank arm at the end of the drive shaft should be made with a 3/8" throw. Install the driveshaft in the driveshaft-mounting block (B) and secure it in place with the crank arm in the horizontal position.

Cut out and drill the holes for parts O and P as indicated on the FS patterns for these parts (Fig. 6.05). The 3/32" holes will accept the wire rods and 5/32" holes are for the #6 screws to be used as pivots. Use #6 x 1" SS

FH pivot screws with a nylon finishing washer under the head and a second nylon finishing washer under O and P. Tighten the pivot screws to secure O and P in their mid-range position. O will be vertically oriented and P will be horizontal. Use 16 gauge galvanized or brass wire connecting rods to link O and P together and to the crank arm of the driveshaft. Measure the assembly to determine the length of the wire connecting rods required to link the parts together. The "Z" bends in the rods can be used to adjust the length of the rods after they have been installed. Install the rods and make adjustments as required. Label and remove the hardware and save for reinstallation after painting has been completed.

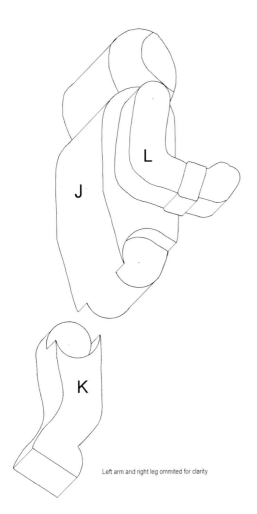

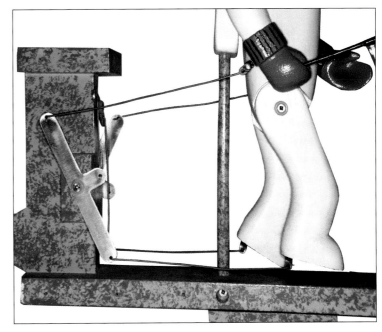

Figure 6.10

Figure 6.09   Left arm and right leg ommited for clarity

Enlarge the patterns for the puppet astronaut shown in Fig. 6.07 to full size and cut out parts J, K, L, and M. Drill pilot holes as indicated on the pattern for the arm and leg pivot screws and a 1/8" hole in the right hand for Q. Mill 9/16" deep recesses with a 1-7/8" Forstner bit on both sides of J and one side of each leg (K) as indicated by the shaded areas on the patterns. Keep in mind that the legs are made as a pair, one right and one left. Fig.6.09 illustrates the half lap hip joints Assemble the hip joints with #6 x 1" SS FH screws. Use two washers between each leg and the body and a finishing washer under the head of each screw. Adjust as required to produce a smooth and effortless motion of the legs. Carve the puppet's body to suit and prepare for painting, leaving a flat area on the puppet's back to which the back pack/ puppet support post assembly (H/N) can now be securely fastened with two screws. Install connectors into the bottom of each foot and at the wrists. Insert H into the hole in A and adjust the height of the puppet so that the legs swing freely without contacting the chassis (A). Secure the position of the post within the chassis with a #6 x 1-1/4" screw in the counterbored hole at the side of the chassis. See Fig. 6.10 for these details. Cut off the lower end of H flush with the bottom of the chassis.

Cut out the cowl from a piece of .025" aluminum using the full size patterns shown in Fig. 6.06. Do not bend the cowl along the interrupted bending lines until after it has been painted. The flag (R) and the flagpole (Q) should be made from brass or copper so that they can be soldered together for durability.

Once construction has been completed, "The Moonwalker" is ready for painting. It will be helpful to disassemble some of the parts to paint them. Refer to Chapter 1 for painting and decorating tips. Apply several coats of clear gloss finish over the painted surfaces to seal the wood and make the paint more weather resistant. Allow the paint to dry thoroughly before reassembly.

The mechanical linkage must be completed before the cowl, propeller, and post pivot are installed. Secure the puppet's arms and legs in their desired mid-range position. Secure the mechanical components on the drive shaft mounting block in their mid-range position. These tasks can easily be accomplished by tightening the pivot screw, which connects the parts to one another. Install 16 gauge wire rods between the connectors on the puppet and P (Fig. 6.10). Test the assembly and make adjustments as required. When you are satisfied that everything is operating smoothly, the cowl and propeller are installed. The position of the post pivot can now be determined and the assembly can be installed. Set-up the completed whirligig on a stand in a breezy location and watch your "Moonwalker" take his first walk on the moon.

Chapter 7

The Jogger

Walking, jogging, and running have become popular activities used to develop endurance and maintain physical fitness. This whirligig was inspired by a remarkable young lady who walks past my home daily, rain or shine, at a brisk pace with weights strapped to her ankles (Fig. 7.01).

The jogging figure is constructed using some techniques already described for the Cyclist. The gait of the Jogger is produced using the mechanism employed by the Moonwalker. Refer to the instructions for these models for details.

The Parts and Materials List (Fig. 7.02) and the patterns for the runner and rudder are shown in Fig. 7.03. I have included alternate patterns for a young male runner (Fig. 7.04), for those craftsmen who wish to make a runner of the opposite gender.

Make the Jogger's body and hip joint using the technique described for the Cyclist (Fig. 5.07). The lower end of K and the upper end of L form the half lap rotating hip joints. Form the 3/8" deep recess into K and L as indicated by the shaded areas of the patterns for these parts with a 2-1/4" Forstner bit in a drill press. Parts K, L, and M must be made as left and right parts of a pair. Use a 3/16" dowel for the hip joint pin. Carve and sand the body, arms, and legs to remove the square edges and contour the body parts. The jogger's arms must swing freely on the #6 pivot screws used to secure them to the Jogger's shoulders. I like to counterbore holes in the arms (M) for nylon finishing washers to be used under the heads of the #6 x 1-1/4" FH SS screws. Use two washers on each screw between the puppet's arms (M) and body (J). Install connectors in the puppet's wrists and feet as pictured in Fig. 6.10.

Dry assemble the puppet's body and legs to test the joints. The hip joints should swing freely without rubbing or binding. Make adjustments as required. Once the joints are operating properly, the puppet's body can be glued and screwed together. Conceal the screws that hold the body together with wood plugs.

Figure 7.01

JOGGER (Parts and Materials)						
QTY	PART	PIECE	DIMENSION (INCHES)			SUGGESTED MATERIALS	NOTES
			T	W	L		
1	A	Chassis	3/4	2-1/2	28	Poplar/Pine	
1	B	Drive shaft mtg. block	3/4	3-1/4	6	Maple/Oak	See Fig, 6.05
1	C	Upper cowl support	3/4	2-1/2	3	Poplar/Pine	
2	D	Standoff blocks (L&R)	1/2	1	2	Poplar/Pine	
1	E	Rudder	.064	10	13-1/2	Aluminum	
1	F	Cowl	.025	11	13-1/2	Aluminum	See Fig, 6.06
1	G	Post pivot block	3/4	2-1/2	4	Poplar/Pine	
1	H	Puppet support post	3/8	3/8	10	Dowel	
1	J	Center body section	3/4	8	9-1/2	Poplar	
2	K	Side body section	5/8	3	6-1/2	Poplar	
2	L	Leg	5/8	3	6-1/2	Poplar	
2	M	Arm	5/8	3	6-1/2	Poplar	
1	O	Reciprocating bar	.064	1/2	2	Aluminum	See Fig, 6.05
2	P	Arm/leg activating bar	.064	1-3/8	4-7/8	Aluminum	See Fig, 6.05

Figure 7.02

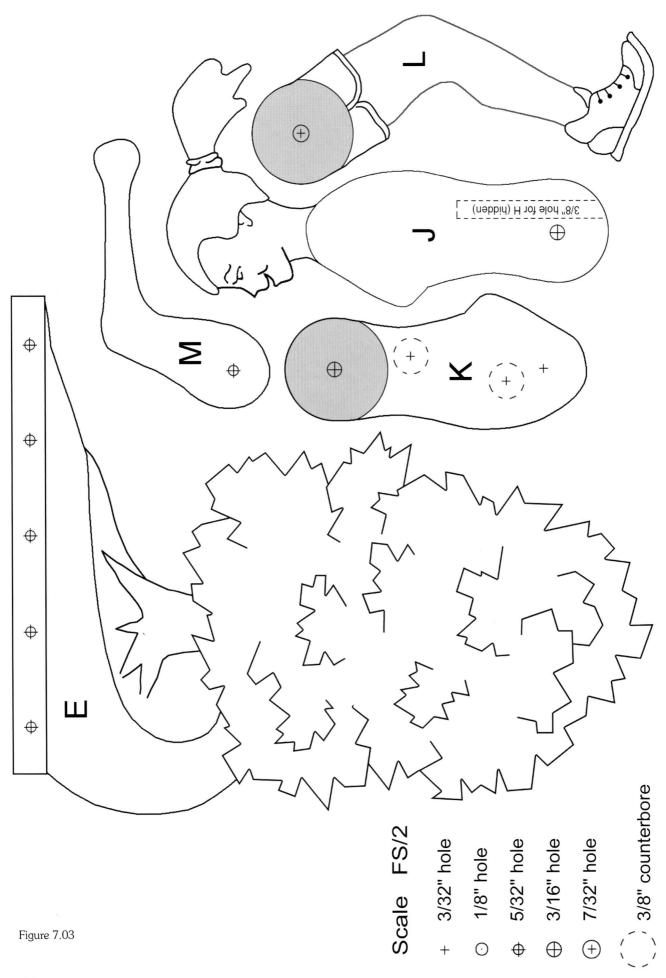

3/8" hole for H (hidden)

L

J

M

K

E

Scale FS/2

+ 3/32" hole

⊙ 1/8" hole

⊕ 5/32" hole

⊕ 3/16" hole

⊕ 7/32" hole

◌ 3/8" counterbore

Figure 7.03

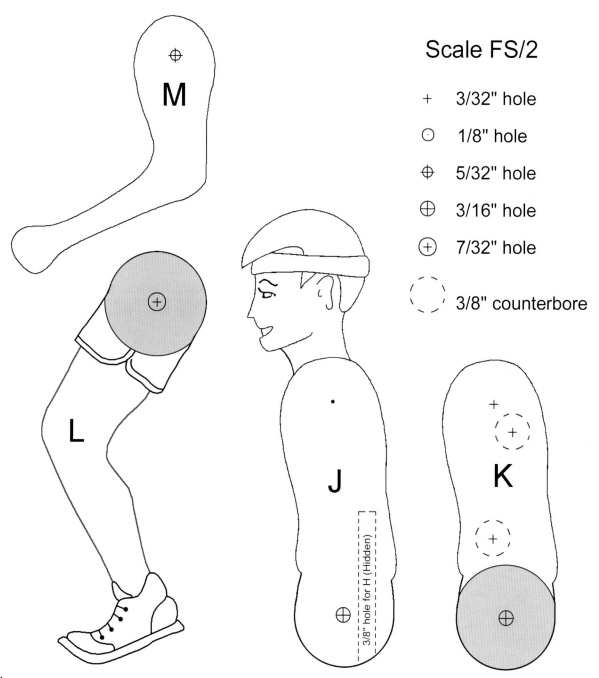

Scale FS/2

+	3/32" hole
⊙	1/8" hole
⊕	5/32" hole
⊕	3/16" hole
⊕	7/32" hole
⊙	3/8" counterbore

M

L

J

3/8" hole for H (Hidden)

K

Figure 7.04

The dimensions for the chassis (A) are provided in Fig. 7.05. Drill a 3/8" hole in the chassis for the puppet support post (H) and a counterbored hole in the side edge opposite this hole for the puppet support post retaining screw. Complete the chassis assembly and install the mechanical components as shown for the Moonwalker (Fig. 6.08 and 6.10).

Adjust the position of the puppet on the support post (H) above the chassis to allow the legs to swing freely. Use a #6 screw in the counterbored hole at the edge of A into H to secure the puppet assembly in this position.

Cut off the protruding end of the support post flush with the bottom of the chassis. Install the connecting rods that will provide the arm and leg movements. Test the entire assembly and make adjustments as required. Remove all the hardware and partially disassemble some of the parts to facilitate painting and decorating.

A propeller with four 9" blades can be used to activate this whirligig. Install a post pivot under the chassis. Make a stand to support the completed whirligig. Details and instructions for these parts are provided in Chapter 1.

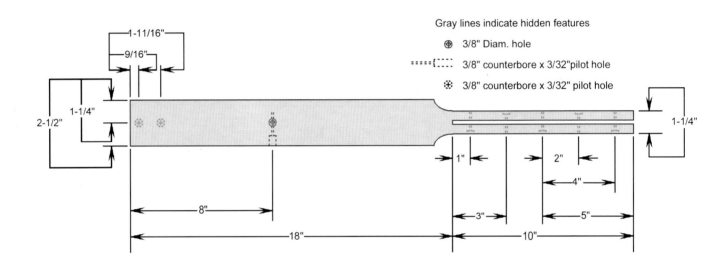

Figure 7.05

Chapter 8
Uncle Sam

This tall, lean gentleman with a gray beard, wearing a red, white, and blue suit and holding a top hat, represents the spirit of the American people. Uncle Sam is an appropriate display for the July Fourth and Memorial Day holidays.

Figure 8.01

Figure 8.02

QTY	PART	PIECE	DIMENSION (INCHES)			MATERIAL	NOTES
			T	W	L		
1	A	Chassis	3/4	2-1/2	16-1/2	Poplar/Pine	Fig. 8.04
1	B	Drive shaft mtg block	3/4	3-1/4	4-3/4	Poplar	Fig. 8.05
1	C	Upper cowl support	3/4	2-1/2	2-1/4	Poplar/Pine	Fig. 8.04
2	D	Standoff blocks (L&R)	1/2	1-3/4	2	Poplar/Pine	Fig. 8.04
1	E	Rudder	.064	7	18-1/2	Aluminum	Fig. 8.04
1	F	Cowl	.025	6-3/4	13	Aluminum	Fig. 8.12
1	G	Post pivot block	3/4	2-1/2	4	Poplar/Pine	Fig. 1.18
1	H	Puppet left side	5/8	5-3/4	12-1/2	Poplar	Fig. 8.09
1	J	Puppet center body	5/8	2-3/4	12-1/2	Poplar	Fig. 8.09
2	K	Puppet right side	5/8	5-3/4	12-1/2	Poplar	Fig. 8.09
1	L	Puppet head	1	2-1/2	3	Poplar	Fig. 8.09
1	M	Puppet right arm	3/4	4-1/4	5	Poplar	Fig. 8.05
1	N	Puppet left arm	1	6-1/2	5	Poplar	Fig. 8.05
1	P	Driveshaft/crank arm	¼" Diam.			Brass	Fig. 1.07A
1	Q	"T" bar	.064	2-3/8	1-7/8	Aluminum	Fig. 8.05
2	R	"L" bar	.064	1-1/2	3-1/2	Aluminum	Fig. 8.05
	S	Pivot screw	#6 RH		3/4	Brass/SS	
	T	Screw	#6 FH		1-1/2	SS	
3	U	Flat washers	#6			Nylon	Fig. 1.12 E
3	V	Finishing washers	#6			Nylon	Fig. 1.12 D
1	W	Head shaft	¼" Diam.		8	Brass	Fig. 8.11
6	X	Connecting rods					Fig. 8.07
2	Y	Connectors	.032	1/4	4		Fig. 1.10
1		Propeller	4 Blades				Fig. 1.03, 1.04
1		Post pivot					Fig. 1.18
1		Post and stand					Fig. 1.22 -1.24

UNCLE SAM (Parts and Materials)

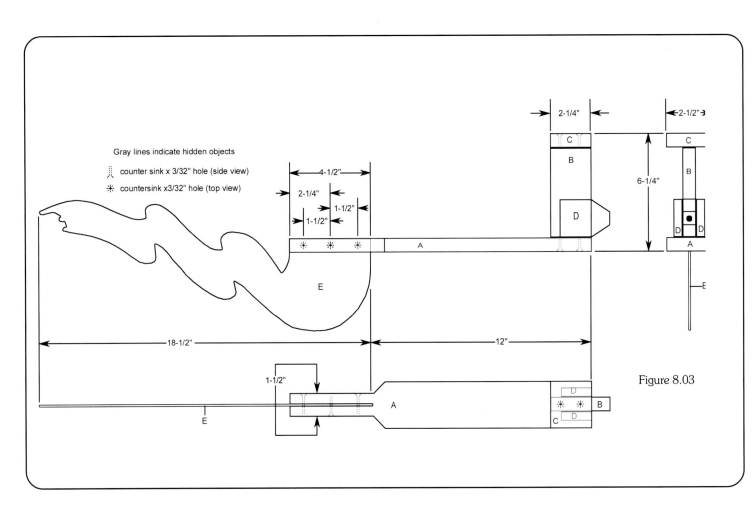

Figure 8.03

Gray lines indicate hidden objects

⌇ counter sink x 3/32" hole (side view)

✳ countersink x3/32" hole (top view)

Construct the chassis assembly as shown in Fig. 8.03. Cut out A, C, D, and E from the appropriate materials using the patterns provided in Fig. 8.04. Cut the slot in A for the rudder (E) before reducing the width of the tail section. Drill and countersink the pilot holes for the #6 x 1-1/4" FH SS screws to be used to secure E to A. Drill 5/32" holes in A to attach B and to connect the puppet's feet to A. Countersink these hole on the underside of A.

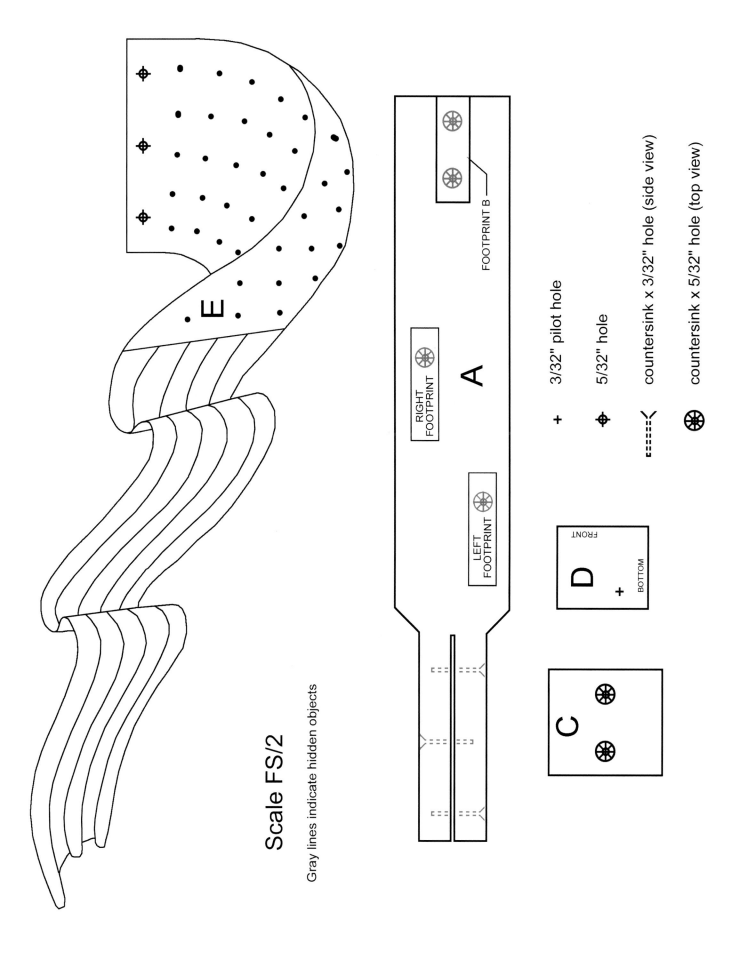

Scale FS/2

Gray lines indicate hidden objects

RIGHT FOOTPRINT

LEFT FOOTPRINT

A

FOOTPRINT B

FRONT

BOTTOM

D

C

+   3/32" pilot hole

⊕   5/32" hole

⋎   countersink x 3/32" hole (side view)

⊛   countersink x 5/32" hole (top view)

E

Figure 8.04

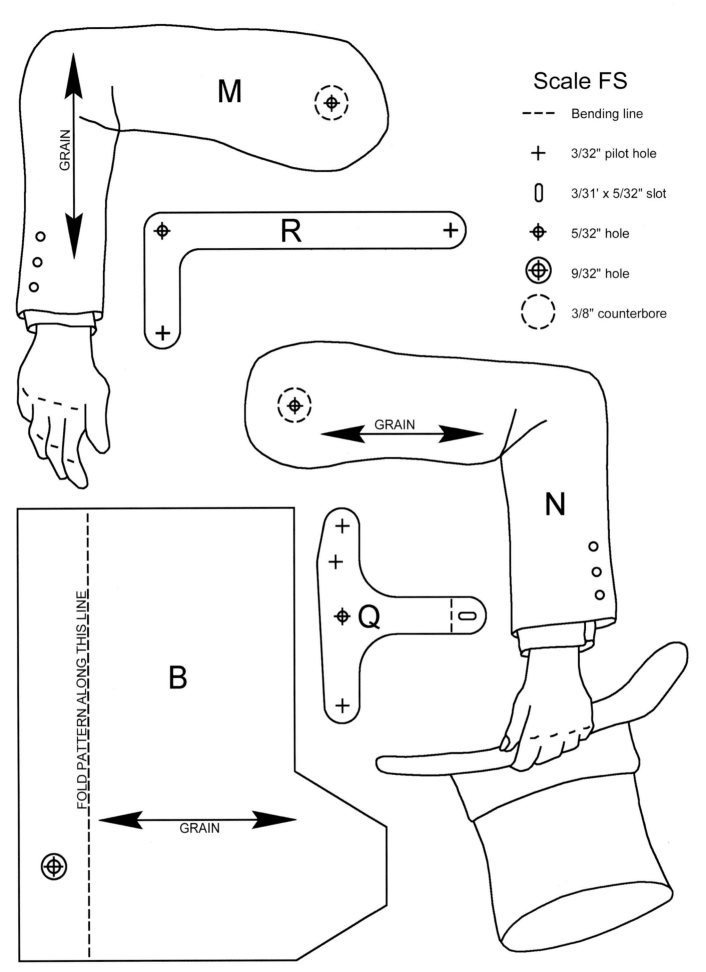

Scale FS

--- Bending line

+ 3/32" pilot hole

0 3/31' x 5/32" slot

⊕ 5/32" hole

⊕ 9/32" hole

◯ 3/8" counterbore

M

GRAIN

R

GRAIN

N

FOLD PATTERN ALONG THIS LINE

B

GRAIN

Q

Figure 8.05

Apply the FS folded pattern of B to the 3/4" x 3-3/4" x 4-3/4" poplar block. Bore a hole for the drive shaft (P) before cutting the block to shape. If you intend to use flanged bushings as bearings for the drive shaft, the diameter of the hole must match the outside diameter of the bushings. Glue the standoff blocks (D) to the right and left sides of B. When the glue has dried, fasten the assembly (D-B-D) to A with two #6 x 1-1/2" FH SS screws. Counter sink and bore pilot holes in C and fasten it to B with two #6 x 1-1/2" FH SS screws in the previously prepared pilot holes. Enlarge the rudder pattern to FS and apply it to a piece of aluminum .064" x 7" x 8-1/2". Cut out the rudder to the outline indicated on the pattern and make the 5/32" mounting holes. Attach the rudder to A with three #6 x 1-1/4" FH SS screws.

Fig.8.06 illustrates the components of the mechanical drive that produce the movements of Uncle Sam.

Use the FS patterns in Fig. 8.05 to make R and Q. Bend the upper arm of the Q and install Q and R as shown in Fig. 8.06. Make the driveshaft/crank arm (P) with a 3/8" throw, as shown in Fig. 1.07A. The threaded end of the driveshaft should extend 1-1/2" beyond the nose of B (Fig. 8.08). Install P in the driveshaft-mounting block (B). Make the adjustable connecting rods as shown in Fig. 8.07. Install X1 between the crank arm of the driveshaft and the inner hole on the horizontal arm of the Q. Connect the outer right hole of Q to the short arm of R (right side) with adjustable wire connector X3. Install adjustable connector X2 between Q and R on the left side in similar fashion. Adjust the length of the connectors so that the crank arm and the Q and R are in their midrange positions as shown in Fig. 8.06. Make two X4's, and X5, and save for future use.

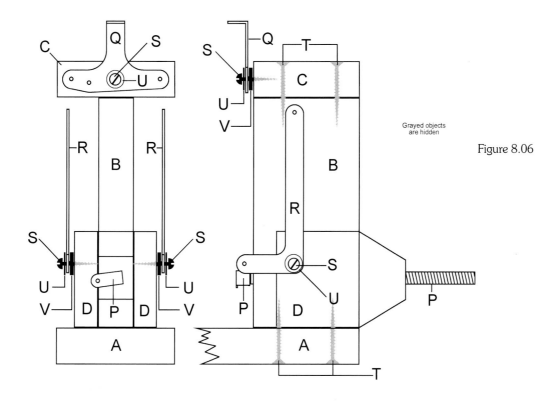

Grayed objects are hidden

Figure 8.06

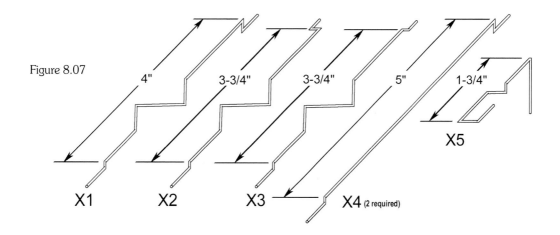

Figure 8.07

X1   X2   X3   X4 (2 required)

X5

53

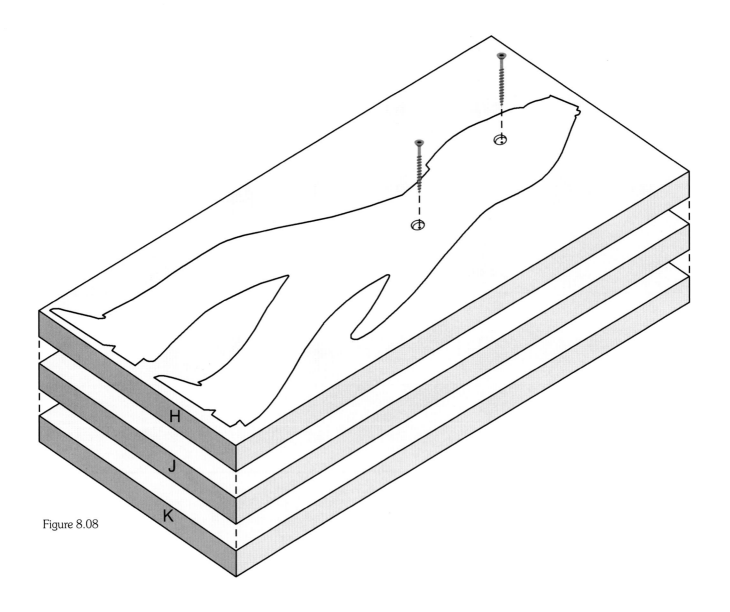

Figure 8.08

H

J

K

Uncle Sam's body is constructed from a block of poplar 1-7/8" x 5-3/4" x 12-1/2" which is built-up from three 5/8" layers (Fig. 8.08). Enlarge the patterns shown in Fig. 8.09 to FS. Secure pattern HJK to the assembled block and gang-cut to the outline of the pattern. Remove the screws from the block and separate the layers. Transfer the patterns of H, J, and K to the appropriate layer and cut off the unwanted parts. Bore a 9/32" hole in J for the head shaft (W). Drill 3/32" pilot holes at the shoulders for the arm pivots and through the soles of the shoes for the screws to be used to attach the puppet to the chassis. Reassemble the block with glue and screws. Use face grain plugs to conceal the screw heads. Carve and sand the body to shape.

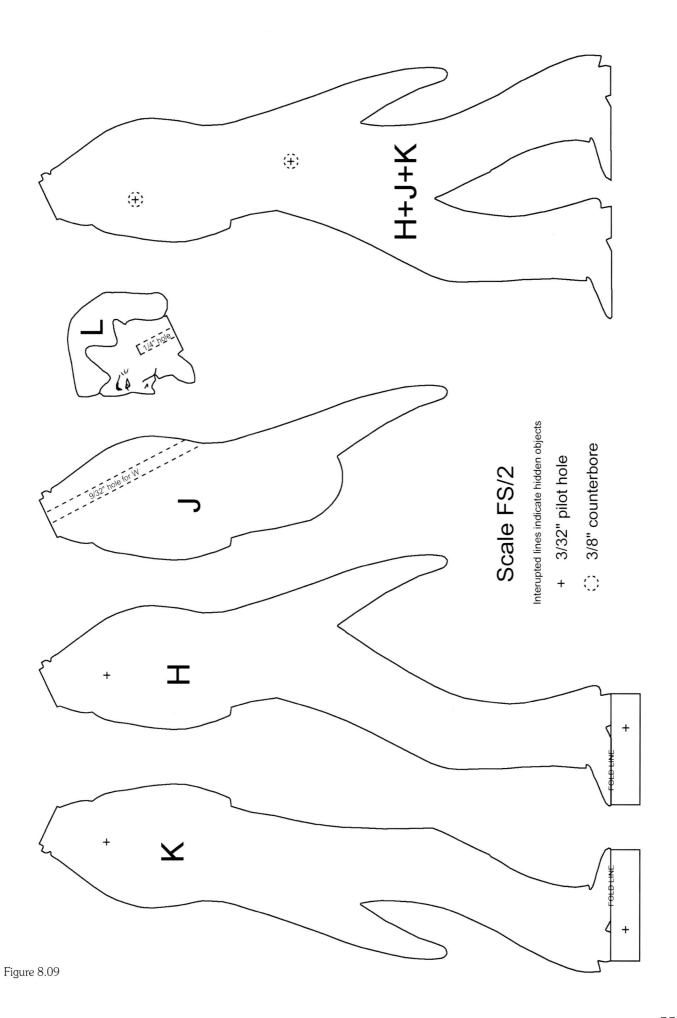

H+J+K

L

1/4" hole

9/32" hole for W

J

Scale FS/2

Interupted lines indicate hidden objects

+   3/32" pilot hole

⊕   3/8" counterbore

H

K

FOLD LINE

FOLD LINE

Figure 8.09

Figure 8.10

Cut out parts L, M, and N. Drill and counterbore holes in M and N for the pivot screws to be used to attach the arms to the body. Drill a 1/4" hole in the head (L) for the top end of the head shaft (W). Carve and sand L, M, and N to shape as shown in Fig 8.01 and Fig. 8.10.

Make the head shaft (W) from a 1/4" x 8" brass rod and make the flange from a piece of .032" x 1" x 1" brass plate with a 1/4" hole in the center. Solder or braze the flange on the shaft. Insert the top end of the shaft into the head with the bottom hole of the shaft oriented left to right and shape the edge of the flange to conform to the outline of the base of the neck. Use two #4 x 1/2" FH brass screws in the countersunk flange holes to secure the head on the shaft. These details are shown in Fig. 8.11.

Partially disassemble the chassis and the puppet as necessary to facilitate painting and decoration. The photographs in this section will be useful as a guide for this operation. Reassemble the parts after painting has been completed.

Replace the hardware (P, Q, R) on the driveshaft-mounting block (B) and reinstall the connecting rods X1, X2, and X3. Adjust as required to produce the desired range of movement from their neutral position, shown in Fig 8.06.

Connect the puppet's body to the chassis with two #6 x 1-1/2" FH SS screws inserted from below the chassis into the legs. Install the head/shaft assembly (Fig. 8.11) in the body with a washer on the shaft between the neck and the shoulders. Install X5 on the end of the shaft and bend over the end to retain. Insert the free end of X5 into the slot in the center arm of Q (Fig. 8.10). Install connectors (Y) into the elbows of M and N. Secure each

arm to Uncle Sam's shoulder with a #6 x 1-1/4" FH SS screw with a nylon finishing washer beneath the screw head. Install connecting rods (X4) between the long arm of R and the connector (Y) on the corresponding arm of the puppet. Adjust as required to produce the desired range of movement. These details can be seen in Fig. 8.10.

The cowl (F) is constructed from a piece of .025" x 6-3/4" x 13" aluminum. A FS half pattern is provided in Fig. 8.12. Duplicate the pattern as shown and as a mirror image to make the opposite half of the pattern. Save the original copy of the pattern, which will be useful when painting the cowl. Secure the copies of the pattern to the aluminum with spray adhesive. Cut the aluminum to shape with metal shears and punch the 1/8" holes for the #4 x 1/2" mounting screws as indicated. The notches at the ends of the bending lines will indicate the position of the bending lines after the patterns have been removed. Paint the cowl as shown on the patterns and as illustrated in Fig. 8.01. Bend the cowl along the bending lines after the painting and decoration has been completed.

Make a propeller with four 1/4" x 3-1/2" x 12" blades and a display stand as suggested in Chapter 1. Once the propeller has been balanced and painted it may be attached to the driveshaft. Balance the completed whirligig along the edge of a board to locate the center or gravity. Install a post pivot mounting block with the post pivot directly beneath the center of gravity. Details of this procedure are discussed in Chapter 1.

Uncle Sam is now ready to take his position on a stand in a breezy, visible location where he will turn his head, tip his hat, and wave his hand to greet visitors as they pass.

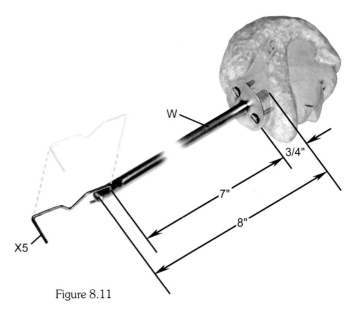

Figure 8.11

FS Half Pattern

⊙ 1/8" hole

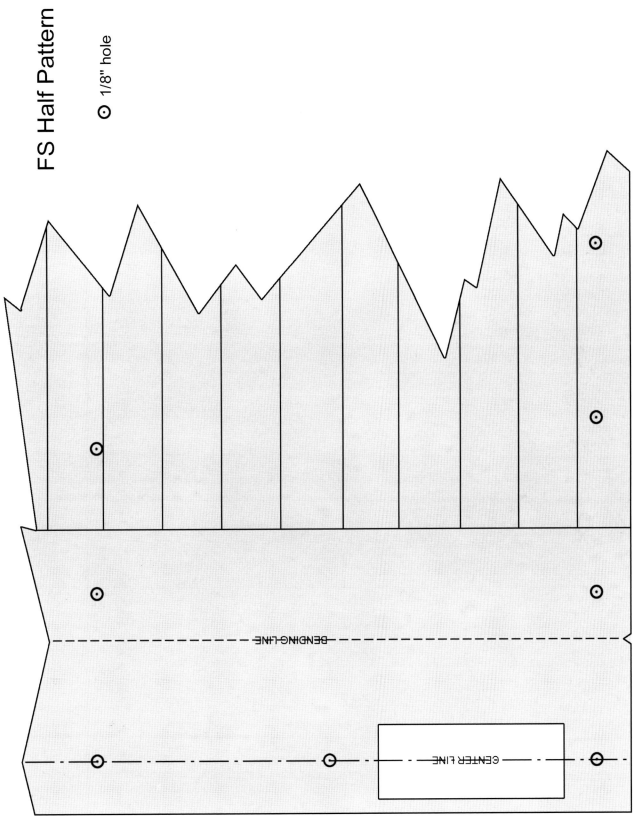

BENDING LINE

CENTER LINE

Figure 8.12

Chapter 9

Bush with a Butterfly

I decided to call this whirligig "Bush with a Butterfly," no political pun intended. Fig. 9.01 shows the completed whirligig, which makes a delightful garden ornament. This butterfly will stay in your garden all summer long.

This project requires metalworking and woodworking skills and allows you to display your artistic talents as well.

Figure 9.01

QTY	PART	PIECE	DIMENSION (INCHES)			MATERIAL	NOTES
			T	W	L		
1	A	Body	3/4	2	7-1/4	Poplar or pine	Fig. 9.08
2	B	Wings	.020	4-1/8	11	Copper	Fig. 9.04
1	C	Chassis	3/4	1-3/4	17	Poplar or pine	Fig. 9.04
1	D	Drive shaft mtg. block	3/4	1-1/4	7	Poplar or pine	Fig. 9.03
1	E	Rudder	.064	8-1/2	9-1/2	Aluminum	Fig. 9.04
1	F	D/S mtg. block cowl	.020	4-1/4	6	Copper/Aluminum	Fig. 9.03
2	G	Side panels	.020	4-1/8	4-1/2	Copper/Aluminum	Fig. 9.03
1	H	Chassis bracket	.020	1-1/2	1-1/2	Copper/Aluminum	Fig. 9.03
2	J	Wing bracket	.020	1/2	1-1/4	Copper	Fig. 9.03
1	K	Guide post	1/4 Diam		7-1/2	Threaded brass rod	
1	L	Drive shaft/crank arm				See Section 1 Drive Train and Mechanical Parts	
2	M	Wing support struts		See Fig. 9.06			Fig. 1.07
1	N	Connecting rod					
5	P	Connectors					Fig. 1.10 B
1	Q	Post pivot block	3/4	1-1/4	6	Poplar/pine	
4	R	Propeller blades	1/4	3-1/2	9	Bass/poplar/pine	

Table title: BUSH AND THE BUTTERFLY (Parts and materials)

Figure 9.02

Fig. 9.02 identifies most of the parts on the cutting list. Fig. 9.03 provides full size patterns for the smaller parts. Fig. 9.04 has half size patterns for the larger parts.

Fig. 9.05 reveals the drive train mechanism and wing support system. Refer to Chapter 1 for a description of the connectors, post pivot, stand, and propeller.

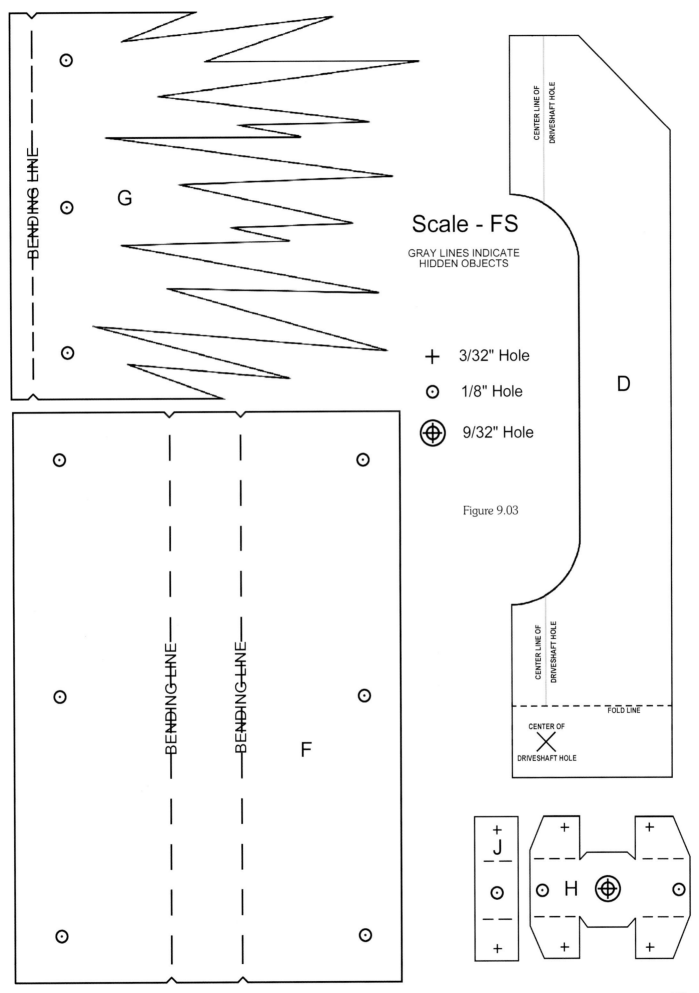

BENDING LINE

G

Scale - FS

GRAY LINES INDICATE
HIDDEN OBJECTS

CENTER LINE OF
DRIVESHAFT HOLE

D

$+$ 3/32" Hole

$\odot$ 1/8" Hole

$\oplus$ 9/32" Hole

Figure 9.03

CENTER LINE OF
DRIVESHAFT HOLE

BENDING LINE   BENDING LINE

F

CENTER LINE OF
DRIVESHAFT HOLE

FOLD LINE

CENTER OF
X
DRIVESHAFT HOLE

J

H

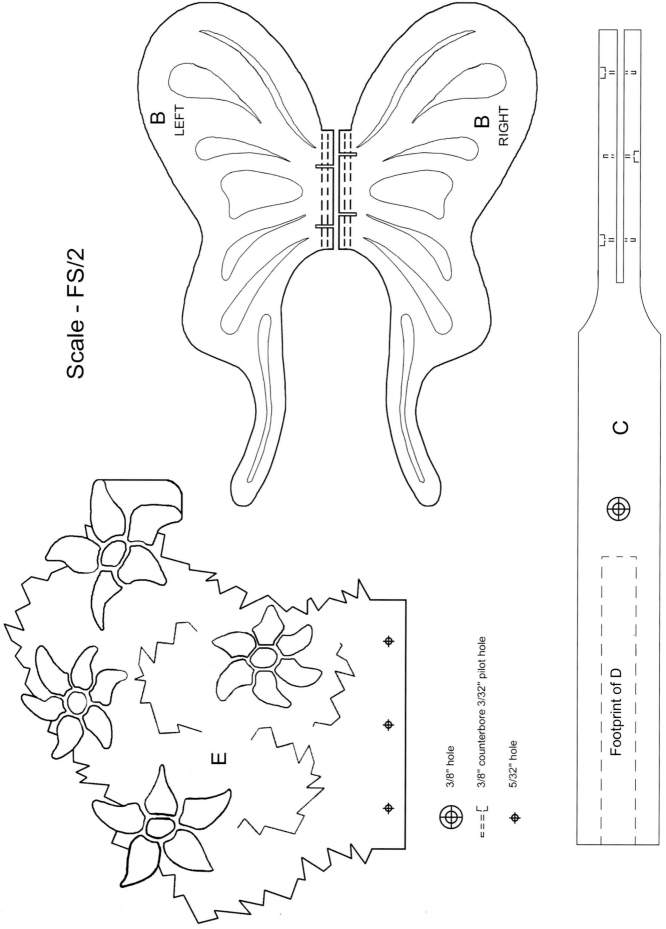

Scale - FS/2

B
LEFT

B
RIGHT

C

Footprint of D

E

⊕ 3/8" hole

⌐⌐⌐ 3/8" counterbore 3/32" pilot hole

✦ 5/32" hole

Figure 9.04

Figure 9.05

Make the propeller with four 1/4" x 3-1/2" x 9" blades (Figs. 1.03 and 1.04). The propeller is secured to the threaded front end of the drive shaft, which ideally should extend 1-1/2" beyond the nose of the drive shaft mounting block. If the threaded end is shorter than the required 1-1/2", counterbore the front of the hub to accommodate the washer and nut used to secure the propeller to the drive shaft assembly. The finished sizes of the drive shaft/crank arm (L), wing support struts (M), and connecting rod (N) are shown in Fig. 9.06. M and N are fabricated from 1/16" brass wire. Solder 1/8" OD brass tubes in the loops formed at the ends of M. Make L as described in Chapter 1.

Because of the excessive length of the drive shaft mounting block (D), it is not possible to accurately drill a continuous hole from front to back. Use a doweling jig to make shorter holes from each end of the block before making the nose taper and center cutout. Bore a hole to match the O.D. of the flanged bearing used with the driveshaft. The cowl (F) will conceal the exposed shaft when it is installed.

Cut out the chassis (C) with a 1/16" wide slot in C for the rudder. The rudder will be secured in the slot with screws in the counterbored pilot holes shown in the pat-

tern. Drill a 3/8" hole through the center of the chassis for a 1/4-20 brass threaded insert, which will accept the threaded end of the guidepost. Install the guidepost (K) and chassis bracket (H) on the chassis as illustrated in Fig. 9.07. Attach the driveshaft-mounting block (D) to the chassis (C) with several screws from below the chassis.

Cut out the pattern (A) for the body shown in Fig. 9.08 along the rectangular outline. Attach the full size pattern to the top edge and sides of a block of wood 3/4" x 2" x 7-1/4" with spray adhesive. To place the pattern in the correct position on the block, align the centerline of the pattern with the centerline marked along the top edge of the block and fold down the sides, as shown in Fig. 9.08. Drill a 9/32" vertical hole through the butterfly's body and cut a 3/32" vertical slot through the butterfly's head. The asymmetrical location of the hinge connectors is identified by the **+** on the right and left sides of the body. Drill 3/32" pilot holes 1/2" deep at these locations for the hinge connectors.

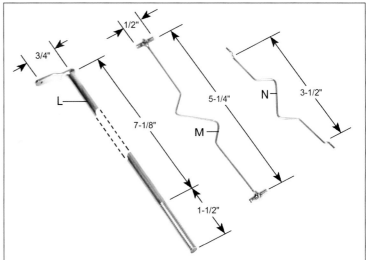

Figure 9.06

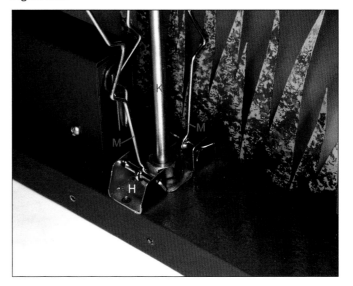

Figure 9.07

61

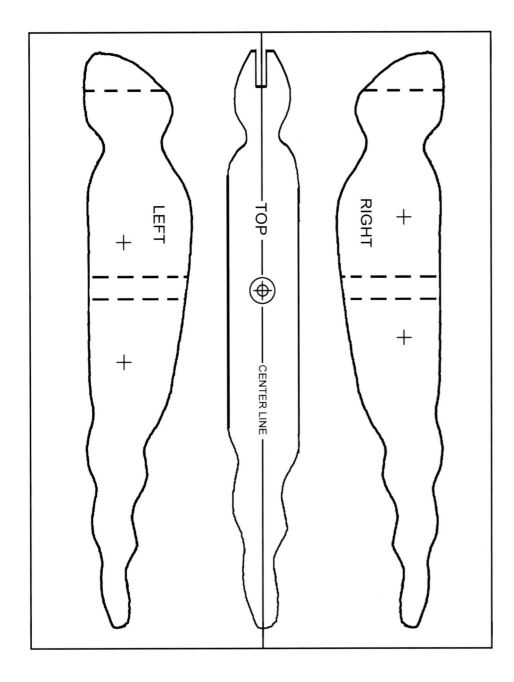

LEFT

TOP

RIGHT

CENTER LINE

With a bandsaw, cut along the left or right profile lines and tack the waste back on the block. Cut along the top profile lines and discard all the waste material. Complete the body contours by carving or filing off the sharp edges and sand the finish contours smooth to prepare for painting. Install the four hinge connectors in the previously prepared pilot holes on the left and right sides of the body after painting this part.

Enlarge the left and right wing patterns to full size. Attach the patterns to the .020" copper material with spray adhesive and cut to shape. Form a channel for the brass hinge tube by making alternate bends along the interrupted lines. Remember that the wings will be made as a right and left pair (Fig. 9.09). Solder a 1/8" OD x 2-1/2" brass tube in the channel. After soldering, remove the sections of the tube that bridge the wings' hinge slots. Temporarily assemble the wings to the body using a 1/16" x 3" brass wire hinge pin with a 90° bend 1/8" from one end of the wire, for each wing.

The butterfly is supported and balanced by the wing struts, which extend from the chassis bracket (H), at the base of the guidepost, to the wing brackets (J). The positioning of the wing brackets (J), on the underside of each wing, is critical if the butterfly is to operate properly. Fig. 9.10 illustrates the procedure used to determine the correct location for the wing brackets under the wings. Line A-A passes through the center of the guidepost hole, perpendicular to the centerline of the butterfly's body and extends out onto the wings. Draw line A-A on the masking tape, which is placed on the wings for that purpose.

Pattern shown FS

Figure 9.08

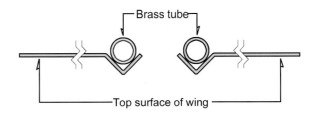

Brass tube

Top surface of wing

Figure 9.09

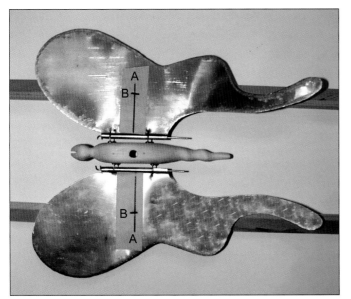

Figure 9.10

secure it in place with several wooden clamps. The paint is applied inside the stencil with a sponge barely moist with paint. Use several light applications to achieve the desired color to prevent excess paint from seeping under the edges of the stencil and creating blotches. Always allow the paint to dry completely before applying any additional layers of paint.

Assemble the whirligig as shown in Figs. 9.01, 9.05, and 9.07. After painting the propeller, secure it on the front end of the drive shaft. Balance the assembly (Fig. 1.19) to determine the position of Q beneath the chassis. Paint Q before securing it to the chassis. Make a stand and post to support your butterfly and set it out in your garden among the flowers.

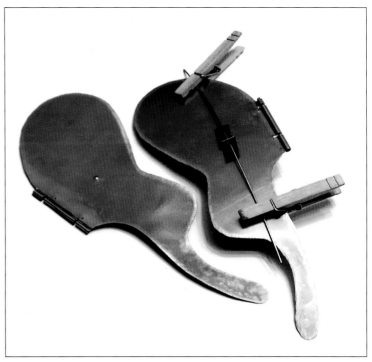

Figure 9.11

Position the body and wing assembly on a pair of balancing beams. Place the beams four inches apart, parallel to one another, and equidistant and parallel to the centerline of the butterfly's body. Adjust the beams by moving them toward or away from one another until the butterfly is balanced with its wings extending horizontally. Line B, which is drawn directly over the balancing beams, will intersect line A on each wing. Make a dimple with a large nail on the wing where the lines intersect. Round over the point of the nail so that it will not perforate the wing surface. The dimple will appear as a small, elevated bulge on the undersurface of the wing, and will indicate the exact position to install each wing bracket. Center the base of each wing bracket over the bulge and clamp it in this position for soldering, as shown in Fig. 9.11.

This whirligig is an interesting project to paint. Most of the parts can easily be painted with a brush or sponge. The designs for the wing (B) and rudder (E), however, are created with stencils. Make one stencil for the purple pattern on the wings. Two stencils are required for the rudder. A small stencil is used to create the branches on the bush and a second, larger stencil is used to paint the flower petals. The stencils are reversed to paint the opposite sides of these parts. Make the stencils by placing sheets of clear plastic over the FS patterns of the wing and rudder. Cut out the patterns using a sharp knife. The stencils can be held in position on the wing or rudder with paper clamps. Fig. 9.12 shows the stencils, stencil knife, and several types of clamps used to hold the stencils in position. After priming, paint the rudder with a dark green base coat. Highlight the edges of the bush with a lighter shade of the same color using a lighter shade of green applied freehand with a sponge. Place the small stencil randomly on the rudder and apply the lighter shade of green to create the branching effect of the bush. Position the larger stencil over the rudder and

Figure 9.12

Chapter 10

Buggy Ride

In the days before Henry Ford mass-produced an affordable motorcar, the horse and carriage was a common means of transportation. A doctor making house calls or a young man and his best girl out for a Sunday ride might have occupied the seat of this handsome buggy. This whirligig is an ambitious project for any woodcarver/metal smith. The drive train for this model will reproduce a realistic gait for the dapple-gray mare pulling this attractive carriage. Fig. 10.01 is a photograph of the completed project.

Fig. 10.03 provides the dimensions and layout for the chassis (A). Cut out the material and drill holes for the screws and support posts (Q) and a 1/16" wide slot for the rudder. Note the counter-bored holes along the edge of the chassis (A) for the screws used to secure the rudder (E) and support posts (Q) to the chassis (A). Drill and counterbore two holes on the undersurface of A for the screws that will join the driveshaft-mounting block (B) to the chassis (A). The interrupted lines indicate the position of B.

Figure 10.01

Figure 10.02

QTY	PART	PIECE	DIMENSION (INCHES)			MATERIAL	NOTES
			T	W	L		
1	A	Chassis	3/4	3	24	Poplar or pine	Fig. 10.03
1	B	Drive shaft mtg. block	3/4	3-5/8	4-1/8	Poplar or pine	Fig. 10.04
1	C	Top cowl support	3/4	3	3-1/8	Poplar or pine	
1	D	Cowl	.020	7	14	Aluminum	
1	E	Rudder	.064	8-1/2	12	Aluminum	FS/2 Pattern
1	F	Carriage shaft	.064	1/2	11-1/4	Aluminum	Fig. 10.09
2	G	Side panels	.020	1-1/2	9-1/2	Aluminum	
1	H	Horse center body section	1-1/4	5-1/4	10-1/2	Poplar or pine	
2	J	Horse side body section	3/4	4	4-1/2	Poplar or pine	
2	K	Horse rear legs	3/4	3	7	Poplar or pine	FS Pattern
2	L	Horse front legs	3/4	1-3/4	6	Poplar or pine	
2	M	Horse ears	.020	Scrap material		Aluminum	
1	N	Horse tail	1/4 Diameter		6	Nylon rope	
1	P	Tail former/retainer tool	.020	Scrap material		Aluminum	
2	Q	Support posts	3/8 Diameter		8	Dowel	
1	R	Drive shaft/crank arm	7/32	7/32	5-1/2	Brass	
1	S	L Bar	.064	2-1/2	3-1/2	Aluminum	
1	T	Guide plate	.032	3	3-1/4	Brass	FS Pattern
1	U	Follower plate	.032	2-3/4	3-1/4	Brass	
1	V	Guide pin	3/32 Diameter		3/4	Brass	Fig. 10.05
1	W	Guide for reins	.020	Scrap material		Aluminum	
1	X	Wire linkage	1/16 (16 gauge)		24	Brass/galv. wire	Fig. 10.06
1		Post pivot block/ hardware	3/4	3	6		Fig. 1.18
1		Propeller assembly	6 blades			See Section 1	Fig. 1.03-06
1		Stand					Fig 1.02

BUGGY RIDE (Parts and Materials)

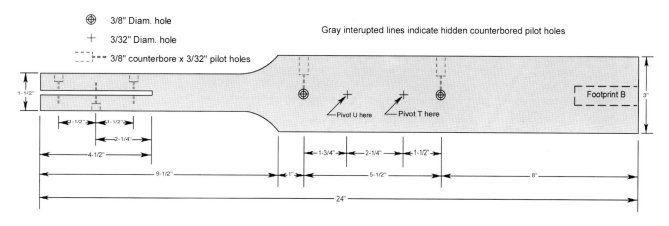

Figure 10.03

Cut out the drive shaft mounting block (B) using the full size pattern shown in Fig.10.04. Bore a 3/8" hole for the driveshaft if you are using flanged bushings, a 1/4" hole if you do not intend to use bushings. I use a dowel jig for this operation. Drill a 3/32" pilot hole for the pivot screw for S. Attach B to A with two #6 x 1-1/4" wood screws.

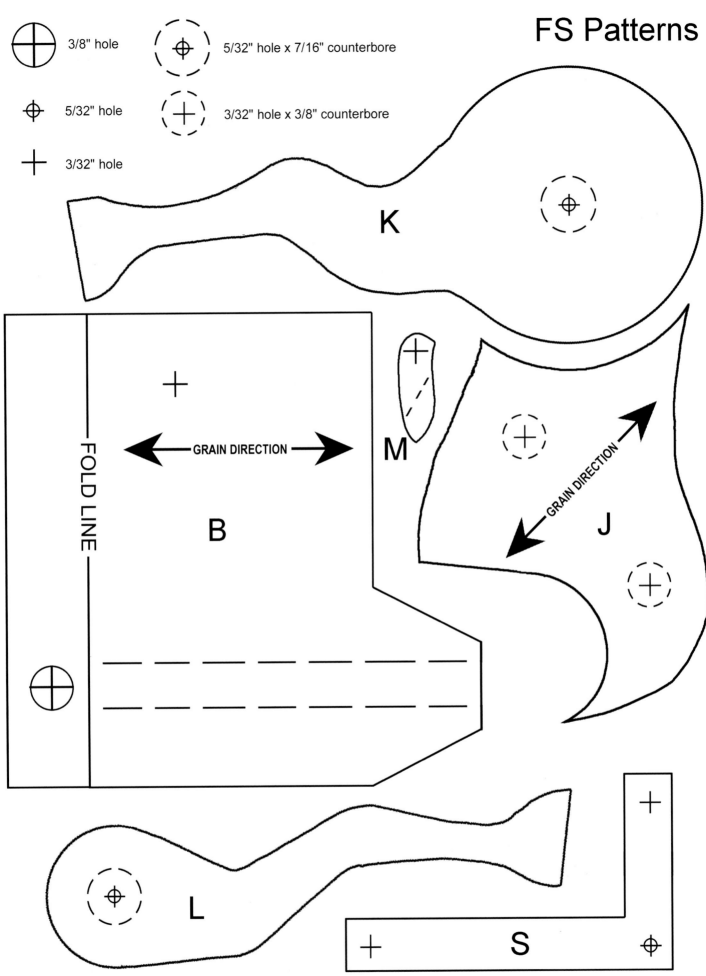

FS Patterns

⊕ 3/8" hole

⊕ 5/32" hole

╬ 5/32" hole x 7/16" counterbore

+ 3/32" hole

╬ 3/32" hole x 3/8" counterbore

K

M

J

← GRAIN DIRECTION →

GRAIN DIRECTION

FOLD LINE

B

L

S

Figure 10.04

Make the crank arm of the drive shaft with a 1/4" throw (Fig. 1.07C). Make parts T and U from .032 sheet brass and S from .064 aluminum using the FS patterns provided in Figs. 10.04 and 10.05. Cut out and file the parts to size. Drill or punch the holes and file a slot for the guide pin (V) as indicated on the patterns. Solder or braze the guide pin to T. Bend the end of the guide pin on T toward U (Fig. 10.06) to an "L" shape. Polish T and U with a wire wheel and bend as indicated by the interrupted lines. Mount T and U to the chassis (A) with #6 x 1" brass round head screws. Attach S to the drive shaft mounting block (B) with a #6 x 3/4" screw and several washers to allow it to rotate freely. Use 1/16" brass or galvanized wire connecting rods with adjustments bends to join the parts. Important features of this mechanical assembly are shown in Fig. 10.06. Notice the guide pin (V) protruding through the slot in U and the position of the connectors under the legs.

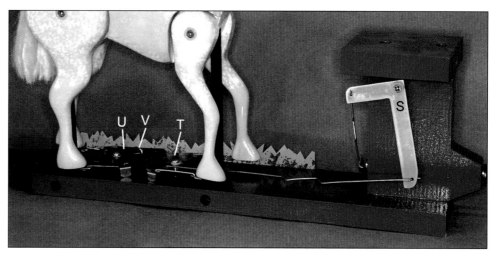

Figure 10.06

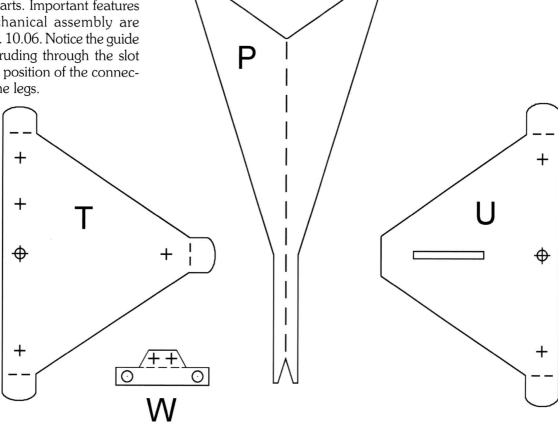

Figure 10.05

Scale FS

+   3/32" hole

⊙   1/8" hole

⊕   5/32" hole

−−   Bending line

Fig. 10.07 is a half size pattern for the center section of the horse (H). Enlarge the pattern to full size. Cut out the pattern around the outside border and fold it along the labeled line. Apply the pattern to a wood block 5-1/4" x 10-1/2" x 1-1/4" with spray adhesive as shown in Fig. 10.08. Drill two 3/8" holes for the support posts (Q), a 1/4" x 1" hole for the tail and two 3/32" x 1-1/4" pilot holes for the pivot screws that will be used to fasten the legs to the horse's body. Cut out the block to the outline of the part with a bandsaw.

Fig. 10.04 contains full size patterns for parts J, K, and L. Gang cut these parts with a bandsaw. Drill and counterbore holes for the screws used to connect the these parts to G. Counterbore the holes, keeping in mind that these parts are to be made as left and right units of a pair. Make a trial assembly of J, K, and L with H to confirm that the legs will swing without interference. Make adjustments as required. Connect J to G with glue and screws and plug the screw holes. Remove L and K. Carve the horse's body and legs and paint all parts before final assembly. Cut out the ears (M) from some scraps of aluminum using the FS pattern. Curl the metal around the interrupted line on the pattern. Paint the ears before installing them on the horse's head with #4 x 1/2" RH brass screws. Attach connectors under the horse's feet as shown in Fig. 10.06. Install the legs (K and L) with #6

x 1" SS FH screws using a #6 nylon finishing washer under the head of each screw and two flat nylon washers between each leg and the body. Adjust the screws so that the legs swing freely. After cutting out and drilling the holes in the rein guide (W) make a 90° bend along the interrupted line. Attach W on the horse's back with two #4 x 1/2" RH brass screws.

Construct and install a tail to complete the puppet horse assembly. Make P from a piece of .010 aluminum (flashing) and bend it along the interrupted line so that the halves intersect one another at about 60°. Make a tassel for the tail (N) by winding white nylon twine around the two notches in P nine or ten times. Insert the narrow end of P, with the twine on it, into the tail hole in H. Cut the twine where it loops over the wide end of P, and part it to expose P. Cut off P as close to the horses body as possible, leaving the narrow end in the hole to retain the tail. Brush the fibers to untwist the twine and create a bushy tail.

Install the horse above the chassis with the guide posts (Q). Adjust the height of the guide posts so that the legs swing freely. Mark and cut off the protruding lower ends of Q flush with the bottom surface of the chassis (A). Secure the posts in the chassis with two #6 x 1-1/4" SS screws in the previously drilled counterbored pilot holes.

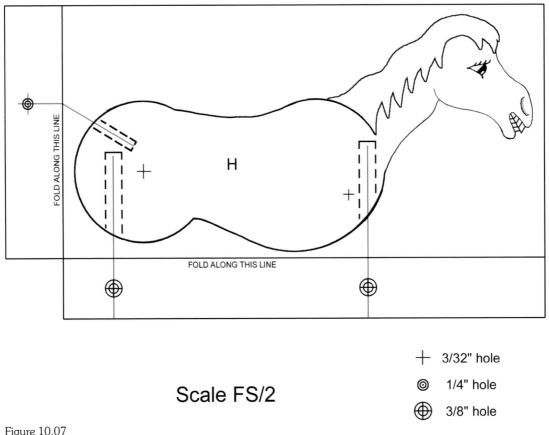

FOLD ALONG THIS LINE

H

FOLD ALONG THIS LINE

Scale FS/2

+ 3/32" hole

◎ 1/4" hole

⊕ 3/8" hole

Figure 10.07

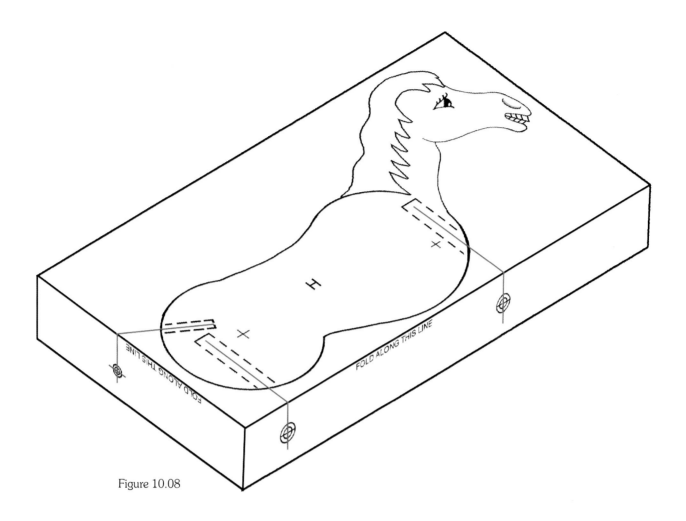

Figure 10.08

FS/2 patterns for the cowl (D) and side panels (G) are shown in Fig. 10.09. Enlarge the patterns to FS and cut out the parts from .020 aluminum. Make 1/8" mounting holes as indicated for the #4 x 1/2" RH screws to be used to attach these parts to the chassis assembly later on. Paint these parts before bending.

Enlarge the FS/2 patterns for the rudder (E) and carriage shaft (F) in Fig. 10.09 to full size. The pattern for F is shown as right and left half patterns with the centerlines and bending lines indicated. File small notches at the end of each bending line to identify their location after the patterns have been removed. Cut out these parts from .064 aluminum and paint before bending. Use #6 x 3/4" SS FH wood screws to attach E to A. Secure D, F, and G in position with #4 x 1/2" RH brass screws.

Make the left and right reins from two 16" lengths of 24 gauge (.025") soft brass or copper wire. Form a loop at the end of each wire that will fit around the shank of the #2 x 1/2" brass RH screws used to connect the wire at the corners of the horse's mouth. Pass the free end of the right wire through the right hole in W and through the hole in the driver's hand from the right side. Pass the free end of the left rein through the left hole in W and through the driver's hand from the left side. Adjust the reins and bend the ends down, as they would naturally drape if they were leather straps.

Construct and paint a propeller with six 1/4" x 3-1/2" x 12" blades as described in Chapter 1 and shown in Fig. 1.03 - 1.06. After installing the propeller, locate the center of gravity (Fig. 1.19) and install the post pivot block and pivot.

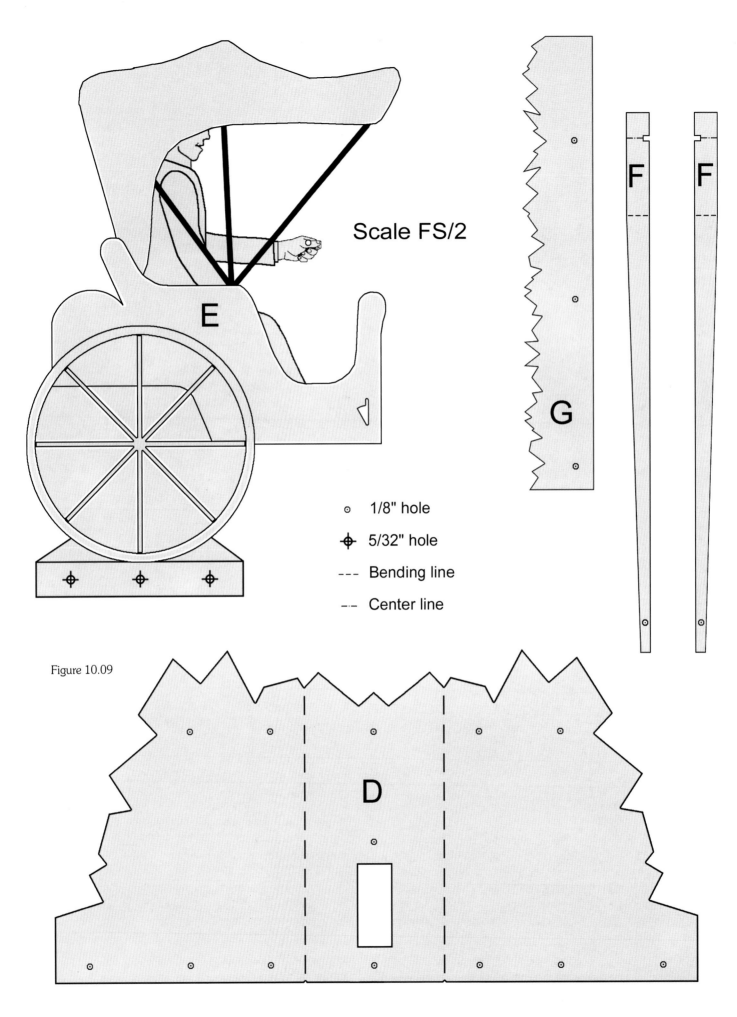

Scale FS/2

E

F   F

G

D

⊙   1/8" hole

⊕   5/32" hole

- - -   Bending line

-·-   Center line

Figure 10.09

Chapter 11
The Concert

Figure 11.01

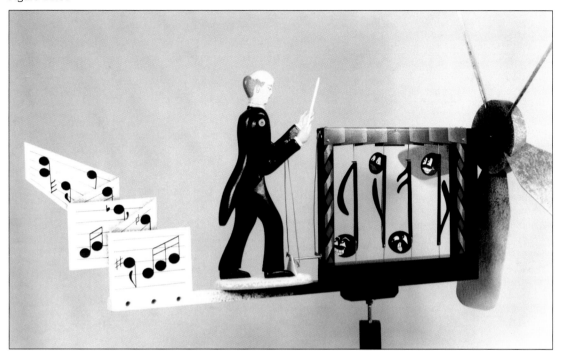

This whirligig represents the performance of a symphony orchestra. The alternate movement of the conductor's arms is in synchrony with the notes, as they change their position on the musical scale. A crankshaft with four offsets produces the individual, alternating movement of the notes while the conductor's arm movements are created by a reciprocating mechanical drive. The velocity of the wind determines The Concert's tempo. Fig. 11.01 is a photograph of the completed project. The Parts and Materials List (Fig. 11.02) and Fig. 11.03 will identify the labeled parts in all subsequent illustrations.

Figure 11.02

QTY	PART	PIECE	DIMENSION (INCHES)			MATERIAL	NOTES
			T	W	L		
1	A	Chassis	3/4	1-1/8	27-1/4	Poplar or pine	
1	B	Front column	1-1/8	3	10-3/4	Poplar or pine	FS Pattern
1	C	Back column	3/4	1-1/8	10-3/4	Poplar or pine	FS Pattern
1	D	Rudder	.064	10	10-1/2	Aluminum	Fig. C.08
1	E	Stage floor	.020	2-1/4	12	Aluminum	FS Half Pattern
2	F	Side panels	.020	1-1/2	11-1/2	Aluminum	FS Half Pattern
1	G	Canopy	.020	3-1/2	11-1/2	Aluminum	FS Half Pattern
1	H-1	Conductor center body	5/8	5-1/4	13-3/4	Poplar or pine	
1	H-2	Conductor right body	5/8	5-1/4	13-3/4	Poplar or pine	
1	H-3	Conductor left body	5/8	5-1/4	13-3/4	Poplar or pine	Puppet assembly
1	H-4	Conductor right arm	5/8	4-1/4	5	Poplar or pine	FS Patterns
1	H-5	Conductor left arm	5/8	4-1/4	5	Poplar or pine	
1	H-6	Conductor's platform	5/8	2-1/2	6-1/2	Poplar or pine	
1	J-1	Bracket	.025	1-3/4	1-5/8	Aluminum	
1	J-2	Short arm	.064	1/4	3/4	Brass	Reciprocal drive
1	J-3	Long arm	.064	1/4	2	Brass	mechanism. See
1	J-4	Shaft	1/8	Rod	2-3/4	Brass	Fig. C.07
1	J-5	Bearing (Optional)	9/64 ID		5/8	Brass	
1	K	First note	.064	2	6-1/2	Aluminum	FS Pattern
1	L	Second note	.064	2	6-1/2	Aluminum	FS Pattern
1	M	Third note	.064	2	6-1/2	Aluminum	FS Pattern
1	N	Fourth note	.064	2	6-1/2	Aluminum	FS Pattern
1	P	Four throw crankshaft	16 Gauge		15	Galv. wire	FS Pattern
4	Q	Suspension rods	16 Gauge		11		Fig. C.12
1	R	Center support	.020	2-1/4	2-7/8	Aluminum	FS Pattern
1	S	Split drive shaft	7/32	Diam.	8	Brass float arm	Fig. C.10
4	T	Lift arms					
1	U	Crankshaft	16 Gauge				
1	V	Reciprocating linkage	16 Gauge				
2	W	Arm linkage	16 Gauge				
1	X	Propeller assembly	5 or 6 Blades			See Section 1 Figs. 1.03-06	
1	Y	Post pivot assembly				See Section 3	
1	Z	Stand				See Section 4 pages 14-16	

THE CONCERT (Parts and materials)

The painting and decorating designs for this project complement the visual effect produced as the conductor's arms move and the notes rise and fall. Notice the pleated canopy and twisted ribbons on the front and back columns that define the stage (Fig. 11.01). Because this whirligig can be viewed from either side, it must be decorated on both sides. Mirror images of the left and right surfaces of each note and the designs for the opposite sides of the rudder appear in subsequent illustrations.

This advanced whirligig project is constructed from a large number of metal parts. It will provide you with an opportunity to develop and practice your metalworking skills. You will have to cut, punch (or drill) holes, fold sheet metal parts, perform intricate wire bending tasks, and assemble metal parts by soldering or brazing. Do not be discouraged if you are unfamiliar with these procedures. Work carefully, follow the recommended suggestions and sequence, and you can accomplish these tasks.

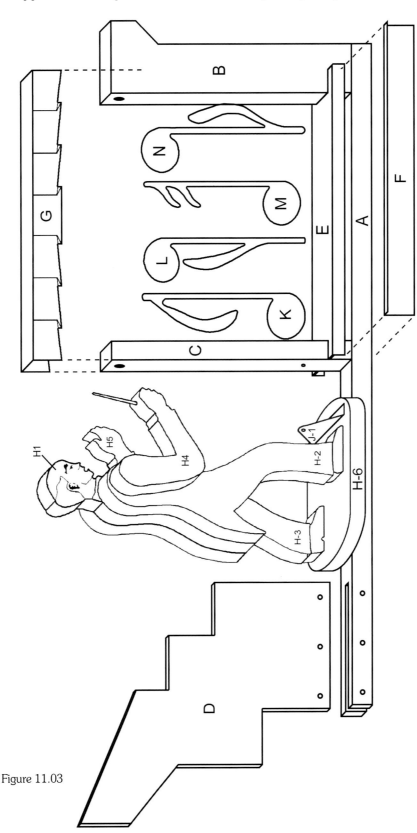

Figure 11.03

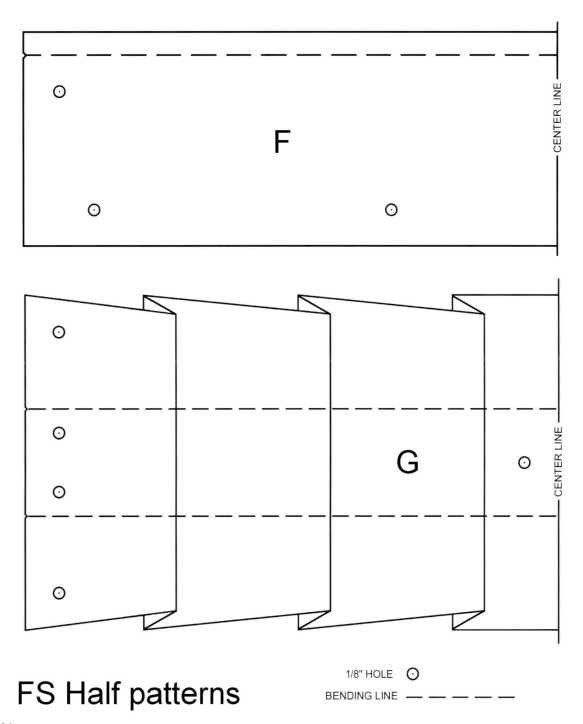

CENTER LINE

F

G

1/8" HOLE ⊙

BENDING LINE — — — — — —

FS Half patterns

Figure 11.04

Start this project by making parts D, E, F, G, J1, K, L, M, N, and R. Patterns for these parts are shown in Figs. 11.04 through 11.08. Secure FS patterns to the sheet metal material with spray adhesive. Use a sharp awl to dimple the material at the center of each hole. After cutting out the parts, file notches at the ends of the bending lines. These notches will accurately locate the position of the bending lines after the paper pat-

terns have been removed. Drill or punch the holes before bending.

Bend the canopy (G) after it has been painted, and then attach the center support (R) to G with two 1/8" blind rivets or small bolts and nuts. Make two side panels (F) using the FS half patterns to lay out, cut to size, and punch or drill the mountings holes. Bend each panel along the interrupted line to form a 1/4" flange.

73

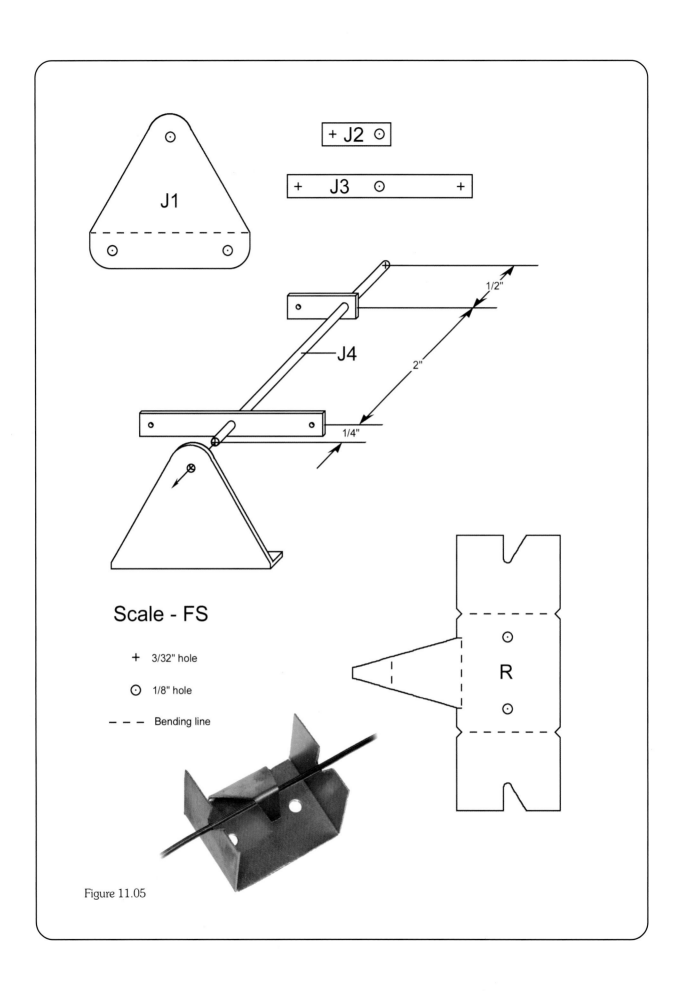

J1

+ J2 ⊙

+ J3 ⊙ +

J4

1/2"

2"

1/4"

Scale - FS

+ 3/32" hole

⊙ 1/8" hole

– – – Bending line

R

Figure 11.05

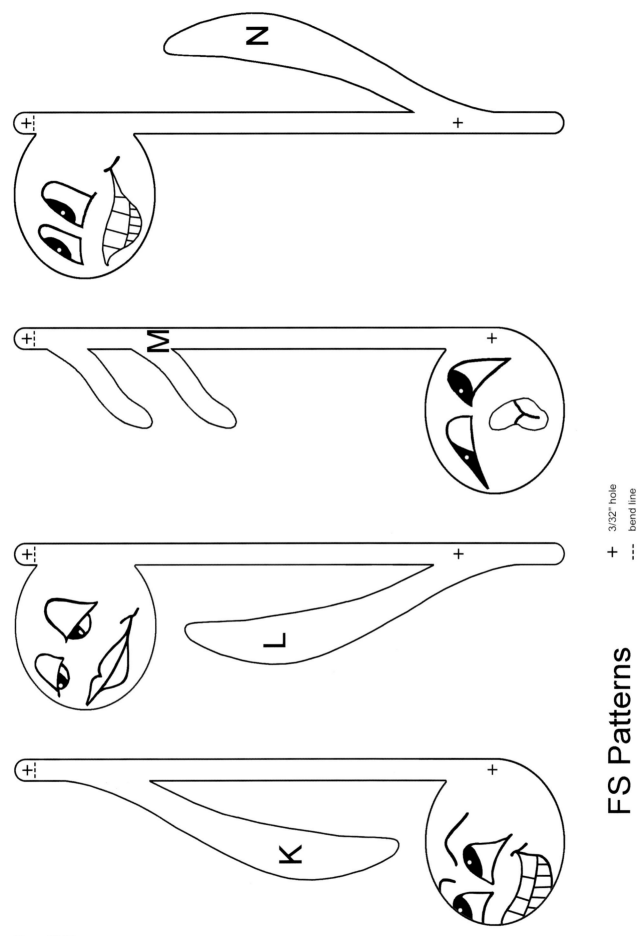

N

M

L

K

+   3/32" hole
--- bend line

FS Patterns

Figure 11.06

75

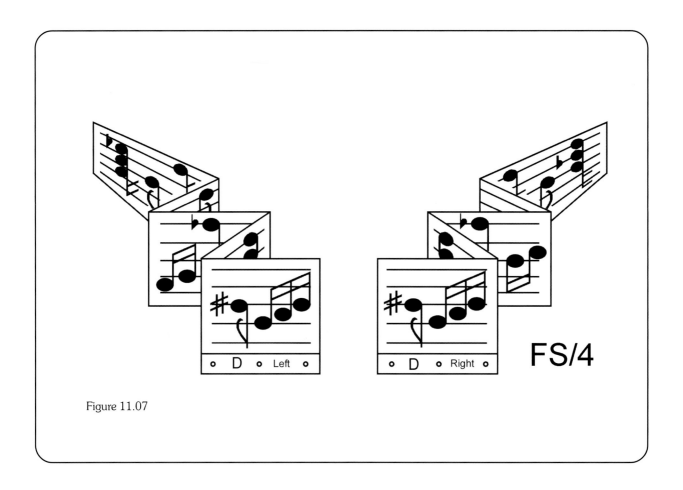

Figure 11.07

Lay out the chassis (A) directly on a piece of wood 3/4" x 1-1/8" x 27-1/4". The length of the 1/16" wide slot and the position of the mounting holes for the rudder (D) can be determined by using the rudder as a guide. Patterns and details for B and C are shown in Figs. 11.09 and 11.10. Bore 3/8" holes in B and C for the split drive shaft/crank arm and its associated bearings. Make 1/4" holes in B and C for the split shaft if you choose to omit the bearings. Drill a 1/8" x 5/8" deep blind hole in C for J4. The bracket (J1) placed on the conductor's platform (H6) will accurately locate the height of the axle hole for J4 (Fig. 11.11). Drill and counterbore the pilot holes in A for the #6 SS FH screws to be used to connect B and D to A. After securing B to A, the stage floor (E) can be used as a jig to accurately position C on A. Mark the location of C and drill and counterbore the pilot holes for two #6 x 1-1/2" SS FH screws to fasten C to A. Se-cure one side panel (F) on either side of the chassis with #4 x 1/2" brass RH screws (Fig. 11.03). Place E between B and C and allow it to rest on the flanges on F. Do not bend the end tabs to secure the stage floor (E) to the flanges of the side panels (F) at this time. Remove E and F from the assembly, paint all the parts, and reassemble. Paint the rudder on both sides as shown in Fig. 11.07 and install.

Attach J-1 to H-6 as shown in Fig. 11.11. Adjust the position of H-6 on the chassis (A) to contain the recipro-cating shaft assembly. Use two nylon washers on the front and back end of the shaft as spacers to allow the mecha-nism to swing freely. Secure H-6 to the top of the chassis (A) with two of the three #6 x 1-1/4" FH stainless steel screws. Remove the bracket (J-1) to insert the third screw under the base of the bracket.

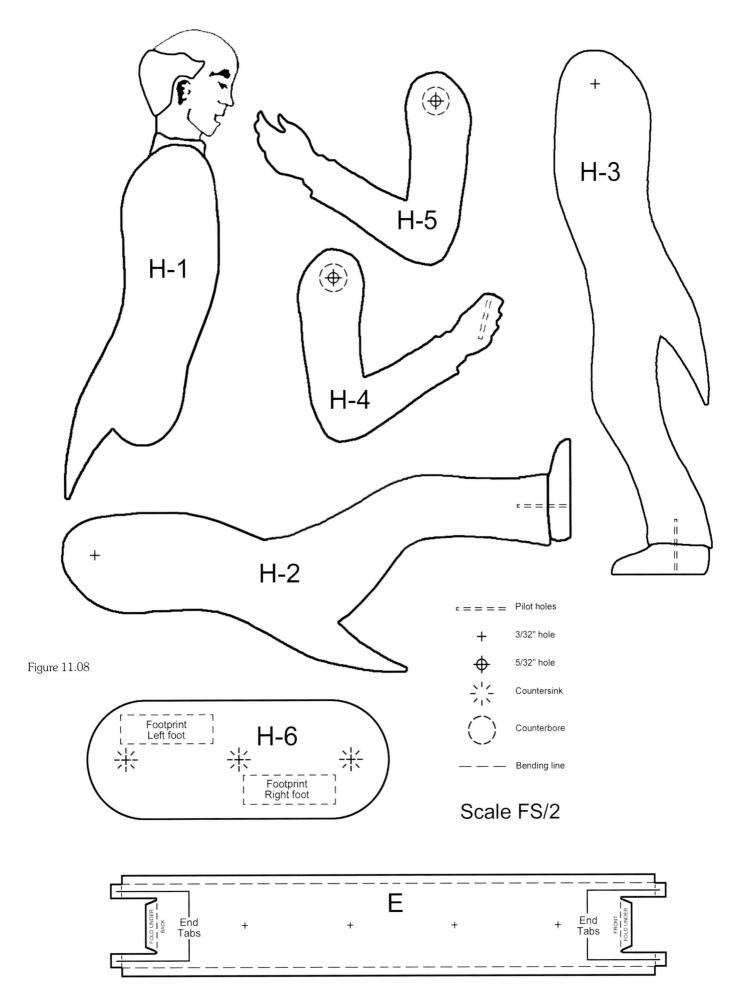

H-5

H-3

H-1

H-4

H-2

Figure 11.08

H-6

Footprint
Left foot

Footprint
Right foot

Pilot holes

+ 3/32" hole

⊕ 5/32" hole

Countersink

Counterbore

Bending line

Scale FS/2

E

FOLD UNDER BACK

End
Tabs

+ + +

End
Tabs

FRONT
FOLD UNDER

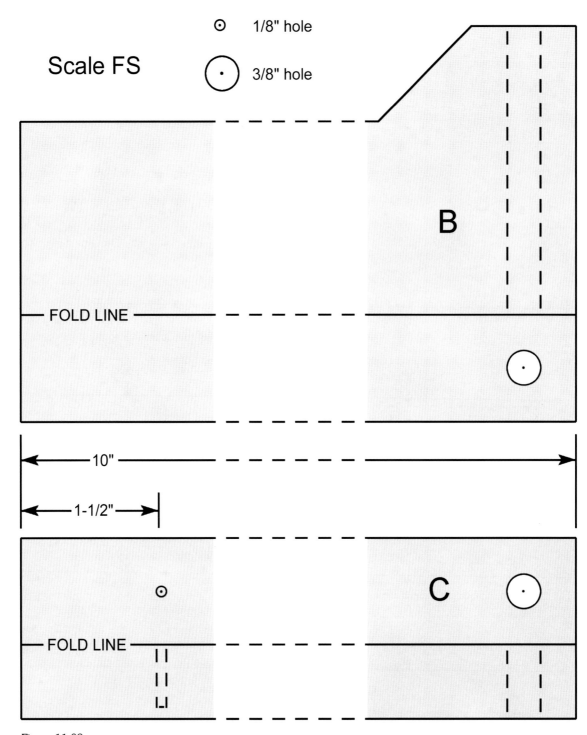

Scale FS

⊙ 1/8" hole

⊙ 3/8" hole

B

FOLD LINE

10"

1-1/2"

FOLD LINE

C

Figure 11.09

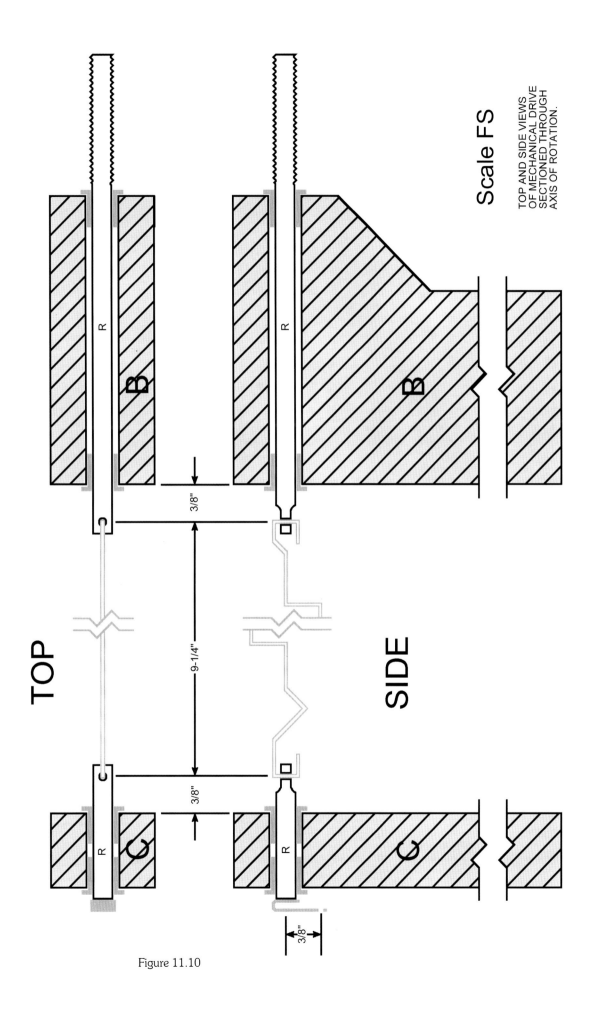

TOP

SIDE

B

B

C

C

R

R

R

R

3/8"

3/8"

9-1/4"

3/8"

Scale FS

TOP AND SIDE VIEWS
OF MECHANICAL DRIVE
SECTIONED THROUGH
AXIS OF ROTATION.

Figure 11.10

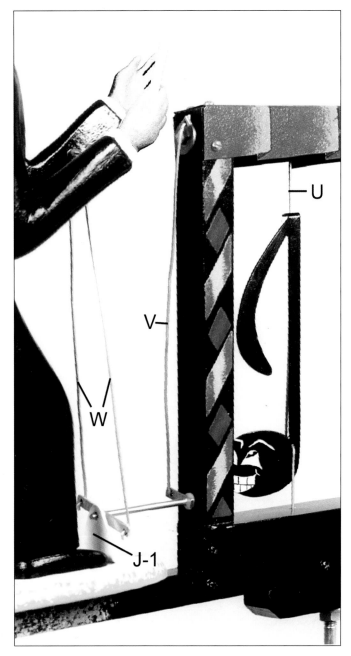

Figure 11.11

Make four suspension rods as shown in Fig. 11.12 Use the jig shown in Fig. 11.13 to hold the brass tube and wire in correct position. Solder the parts together.

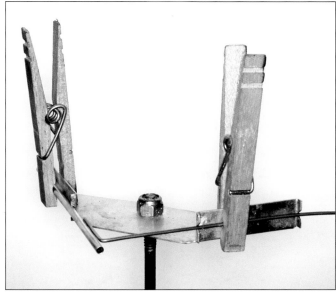

Figure 11.13

Form the four throw crankshaft (P) from a piece of 16 gauge galvanized wire. Start bending at the center and work towards the ends, using the FS drawing (Fig. 11.14) as a guide. Add the suspension rods (Q) before you complete each offset bend. Note the orientation of the suspension rods on the crankshaft as shown in Fig. 11.15. Make a trial assembly of the four-throw crankshaft with the split drive shaft in the chassis assembly. When the canopy is in position, the center support bracket (R) will prevent the crankshaft from sagging in the middle. Each suspension rod wire must pass through its corresponding hole in the stage floor (E). Cut off the ends of each suspension wire 1-1/4" below the stage floor when in its highest position. Test the mechanism and adjust as required. Install the notes (K, L, M, and N) on the suspension rods after painting (Fig. 11.16) as shown in Fig. 11.11. Position the notes on the suspension rods so that they are 3/8" above E at their lowest position.

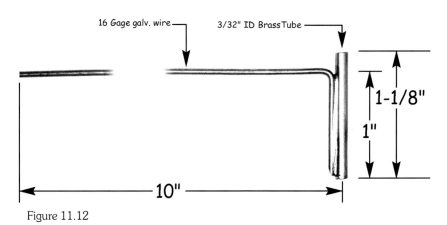

Figure 11.12

16 Gage galv. wire 3/32" ID Brass Tube

1-1/8"

1"

10"

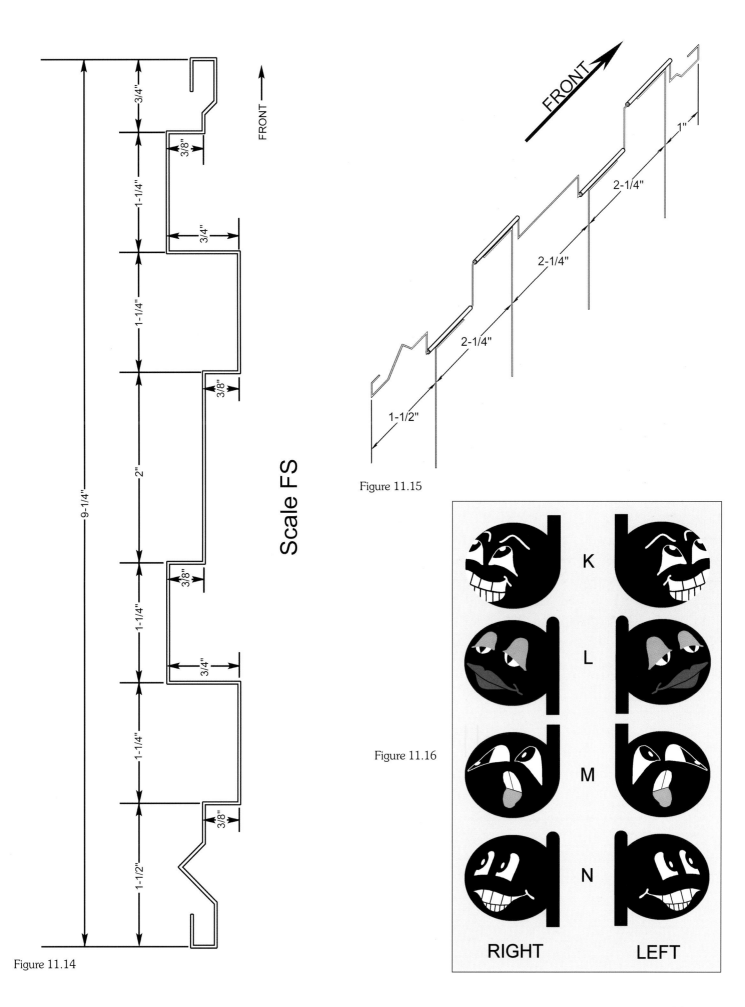

Scale FS

Figure 11.14

Figure 11.15

Figure 11.16

RIGHT   LEFT

81

The body of the puppet conductor is constructed from layers as shown in Fig. 11.03. A FS/2 pattern of the puppet body profile is provided in Fig. 11.17. Enlarge this pattern to FS and secure it to the block as shown. Gang cut the stack to this outline. Separate the blocks. Cut off the unwanted parts to complete H1, H2, and H3 using the individual patterns (Fig. 11.08) as a guide. The arms (H-4 and H-5) pivot at the shoulders on the #6 x 1-1/4" FH stainless steel screws, which connect them to the body. The 5/32" clearance holes for these screws are counterbored to accommodate #6 nylon finishing washers under the heads of the pivot screws. Use two nylon washers on the shank of each pivot screw between the arm and the body. The conductor's baton can be made from a small dowel or metal rod and inserted into a pre-drilled hole in the conductor's right hand. Drill 3/32" pilot holes up into the legs for the #6 x 1-1/4" SS FH screws used to connect the puppet to the platform (H-6). These details are shown on the patterns in Fig. 11.08.

Remove the arms from the body to carve and paint the puppet. Install the puppet on H-6 with two #6 x 1-1/2" SS FH screws. Add an adjustable connecting rod (T) between the crank arm of the split drive shaft and the short arm (J2) of the reciprocating mechanism. Use two connecting rods (U) from the long arm (J3) to the conductor's right and left arms. See Fig. 11.11 and 11.18 for details. Test and adjust the mechanism as required.

Make a propeller with five or six 1/4" x 3-1/2" x 12" blades as described in Chapter 1 and shown in Figs. 1.03-1.06. Install the propeller after painting. Balance the whirligig to determine its center of gravity (Fig. 1.19). Install a post pivot block and pivot directly below the center of gravity. Construct a post and stand to display this whirligig as suggested in Chapter 1 (Figs. 1.22-1.24) to complete this project.

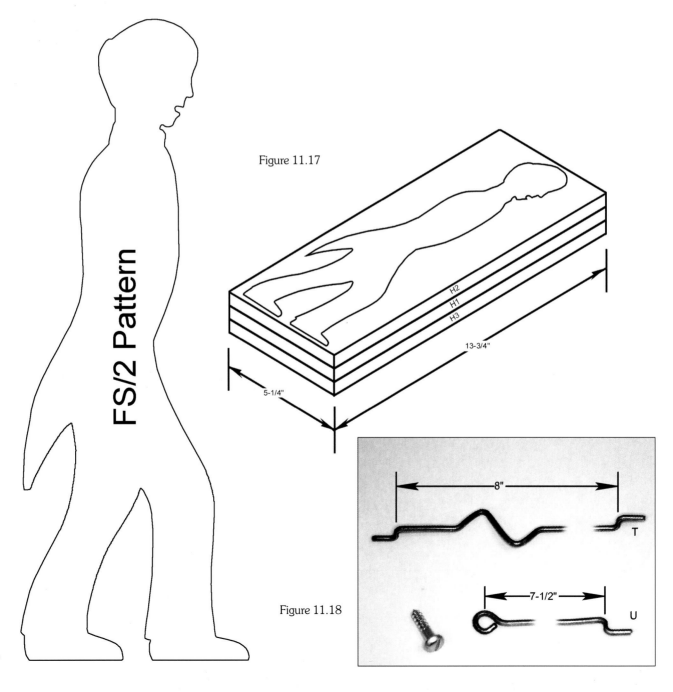

FS/2 Pattern

Figure 11.17

H2
H1
H3

13-3/4"

5-1/4"

8"

T

7-1/2"

U

Figure 11.18

Chapter 12
Planetary Exploration

NASA's planetary exploration program is responsible for launching unmanned spacecraft to gather data about our neighboring planets. The whirligig pictured in Fig. 12.01 represents the launch of one such rocket ship. The spinning propeller is painted to suggest the sun. The moon around the destination planet makes its rotation more apparent. The remaining design features require no explanation. This composition features the use of some new ideas, materials, and techniques for whirligig construction. Fabrication of the sphere is accomplished with plaster cloth, a familiar material for model railroad enthusiasts, and a new material for whirligig builders. The rotational movement of the planet is produced by a sprocket and cogwheel mechanism constructed with bearings to minimize friction.

The labeled parts shown in the illustrations that follow can be identified using the parts list (Fig. 12.02) where they are described by name, size, and composition.

Figure 12.01

Figure 12.02

PLANETARY EXPLORATION (Parts and Materials)							
			DIMENSION (INCHES)			MATERIAL	NOTES
QTY	PART	PIECE	T	W	L		
1	A	Chassis	3/4	2	22-1/4	Poplar or pine	Fig. 12.04
1	B	Drive shaft mtg. block	3/4	2	4-1/2	Poplar or pine	Fig. 12.05
1	C	Front cowl support	3/4	2	3-1/8	Poplar or pine	Fig. 12.05
1	D	Side cowl support	3/4	1	9	Poplar or pine	
1	E	Cowl	.020	4	30-1/2	Aluminum	Fig. 12.04
1	F	Rudder	.064	12	15-1/4	Aluminum	Fig. 12.03
1	G	Planet assembly	8" diameter sphere			Plaster cloth	Fig. 12.06-12.07
1	H	Post pivot mtg. block	3/4	2	6	Poplar or pine	
1	J	Propeller assembly	6 blades				Fig. 1.03-1.06
1	K	Cogwheel	3/4	6-5/8 Diameter		Poplar or pine	Cog wheel assembly Fig. 12.09
32	L	Cogs	#6		1-1/2	Brass screws	
4	M	Cogwheel clips	.020	1-3/4	2-3/4	Brass	
1	N	"T" Nut	5/16-18			Stainless steel	
1	P	Cogwheel pivot	5/16-18 x 4			Stainless steel	
1	Q	Flanged bushing	5/16 I.D.		1/2	Bronze	
1	R	Pivot bearing	7/16 Diameter		1/2	Brass	
1	S	Washer	3/8 I.D.			Stainless steel	
1	T	Nut	5/16-18			Stainless Steel	
1	U	Drive shaft	7/32 Diameter		6-5/8	Brass	Fig. 12.11
1	V	Sprocket gear	.032	1-9/16 Diameter		Brass	Fig. 12.10
4	W	Spacer washer	1/4 I.D.			Brass	
1	X	Moon	1-1/2" Diameter			Foam ball	
1	Y	Post pivot assembly					Fig. 1.18
1	Z	Stand					Fig. 1.22-1.24

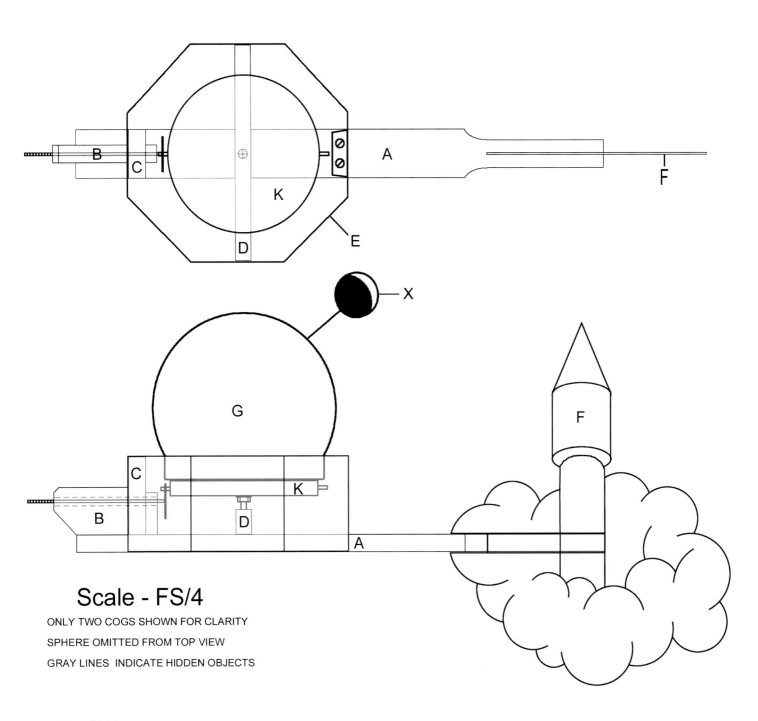

Scale - FS/4

ONLY TWO COGS SHOWN FOR CLARITY

SPHERE OMITTED FROM TOP VIEW

GRAY LINES INDICATE HIDDEN OBJECTS

Figure 12.03

Begin construction with the chassis assembly (A, B, C, D, E) shown in Fig. 12.03. Enlarge the patterns in Fig. 12.04 to full size. Cut a piece of pine or poplar to the dimensions provided in the parts list for A. Secure the front section of the chassis pattern to one end of the material and the back section of the pattern to the other end with spray adhesive. Bore a 7/16" hole for the cog-wheel pivot. Drill and counterbore the six 5/32" holes for the #6 x 1-1/4" SS screws to be used to connect B, C, and D to the chassis. Cut a 1/16" wide slot in the chassis for the rudder before reducing the width of the rudder section to 1". Drill and counterbore 3/32" pilot holes through the edge of the tail section for the #6 x 3/4" SS FH screws to be used to attach the rudder (F) to the chassis. Make a 1/16" deep kerf on each edge of the chassis for the cowl as indicated on the front section of the pattern. These slots will receive the lower inside edge of the cowl's front panel cutout.

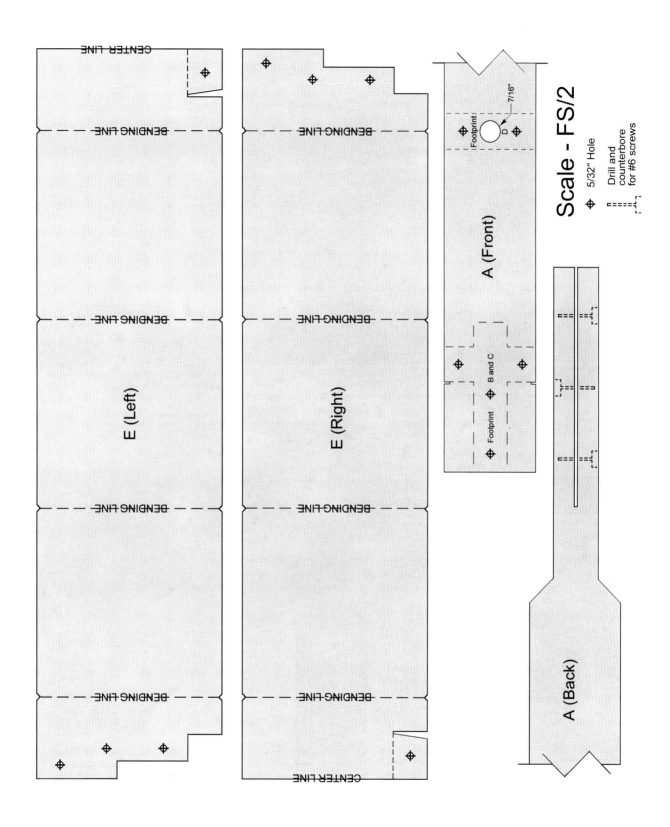

Figure 12.04

DRIVE SHAFT MOUNTING BLOCK (B)

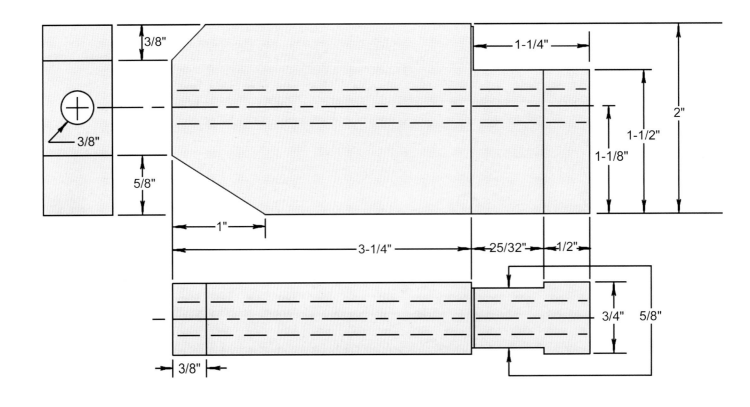

FRONT COWL SUPPORT (C)

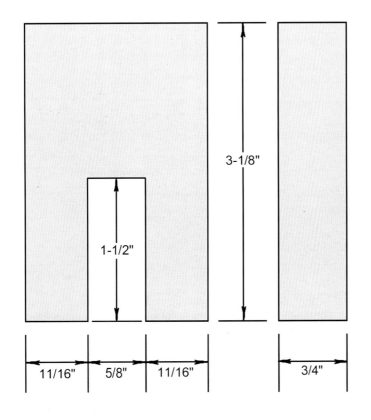

Scale - FS

Figure 12.05

Cut out parts B, C, and D as shown in Fig. 12.05. Assemble B, C, and D with #6 SS screws. Extend the 7/16" hole in A through D.

Make an aluminum panel .020" x 4" x 30-1/2" and secure the left and right FS cowl patterns to it with spray adhesive. Drill or punch the eight 5/32" holes as indicated on the patterns. File small notches at the ends of each bending line. These notches will indicate the position of the bending lines after the patterns have been removed. Paint the cowl before bending it into its octagonal shape. Bend the mounting tab in the back panel forward into the open center of the cowl. Fasten the cowl (E) to C and A with #6 x 5/8" RH SS screws through the mounting holes. Use similar screws to secure the cowl to the ends of D after locating and making 5/32" mounting holes in the side panels of E for this purpose.

Fabrication of the hollow sphere will provide an opportunity to use a new material and technique. Make the plaster cloth sphere on the form shown in Fig. 12.06. A strip of aluminum flashing 3-1/2" x 23" is covered with masking tape along one edge and formed into a cylinder 7" in diameter. The joint where the ends overlap is also taped. The tape will prevent the sharp edges of the aluminum from cutting the balloon. The base of the form is a platform of plywood 9" x 9" with a 3/4" x 7" diameter disc attached in the center. Drill two 1/4" holes about 1-1/2" apart on either side of the disc's center and through the platform. Inflate a round balloon to 8" in diameter and tie it closed with a piece of string, leaving two long ends. Place the aluminum cylinder over the disc and secure it in place by tying the balloon over it. Secure the balloon on top of the aluminum cylinder by passing each end of the string through a hole in the base, and tying the ends together beneath the platform.

Figure 12.06

Cut the plaster cloth into strips about 2" x 4" and apply the strips over the balloon and down over the aluminum cylinder about 2", until the material is about 1/8" thick. Follow the directions on the plaster cloth package. Do not smooth the plaster cloth excessively during application. An uneven, irregular surface will create a more realistic reproduction of the planet's surface. Allow the material to set overnight. Before removing the plaster cloth sphere from the form, use a surface gauge to scribe a line around the cylinder to mark a 1" high collar at the base of the sphere (Fig. 12.07). Disassemble the form and remove the sphere. Cut off the excess plaster cloth material below the scribed line. Paint the globe with several coats of acrylic gesso and decorate it with acrylic paint. Seal the outer and inner surfaces of the globe with several coats of clear gloss acrylic varnish. The acrylic paint and varnish will produce a weather resistant finish on the plaster cloth sphere. After painting G, the moon (X) may be installed. It is made from a plastic foam ball 2" in diameter to which a 16-gauge wire support has been attached. The surface of the moon should be sealed with acrylic gesso and clear gloss acrylic varnish.

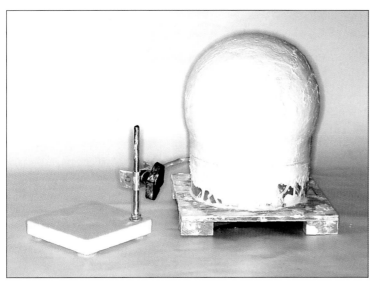

Figure 12.07

Fabrication of the cogwheel mechanism requires precise layout, cutting, and drilling. Mark the center of the material to be used for the cogwheel (K) by drawing two perpendicular, intersecting lines on the top surface. Drill and counter bore the center hole for a 5/16" - 18 nut (T) and washer (T). Use a short bolt as a center guide and cut out the 6-5/8" diameter cogwheel on a bandsaw. Layout the pilot holes for the 32 cogs carefully. To accomplish accurate positioning, the following method is suggested. Cut a strip of heavy craft paper   3/4" wide x 24" long. Wrap the paper around the edge of the cogwheel. Mark and cut the paper strip to the exact circumferential dimension of your wheel. Fold the strip into quarters. Divide the strip into thirty-two equal parts us-

ing the method described in Fig. 1.17. Use this strip of paper to layout the cog intervals along the edge of the cogwheel one quarter of the circumference at a time. Use the jig shown in Fig. 12.08 to hold the cogwheel vertically on edge and drill 3/32" pilot holes for the cogs with a drill press.

Make the cogs (L) by cutting off the heads of #6 x 1-1/2" brass screws and rounding over their cut ends. After painting the cogwheel, install the cogs with a driver drill until only 3/8" of the shank is exposed. Install the cogwheel pivot (P) in the center hole of the cogwheel using a "T" nut (N), washer (S), and hex nut (T) as shown in Fig. 12.09. Install four cogwheel clips (M) on the cogwheel to hold the hollow sphere in place. FS patterns for the clips are shown in Fig. 12.10.

The drive shaft (U) is made from a 7/32" brass rod with extruded 1/4 - 20 threads. The unthreaded portion of the drive shaft must be long enough to accommodate the drive shaft mounting block (B), flanged bushings (Q), four spacer washers (W), and an additional   1/8". The additional 1/8" extension of the shaft is turned down to 5/32" in diameter with a shoulder (Fig. 12.11). Cut out the five-sprocket gear (V) using the full size pattern provided in Fig. 12.10. Make the wheel from a piece of .032 brass and punch or drill a 5/32" hole in the center. Place the sprocket gear over the turned down end of the drive shaft and solder or braze the parts together. Keep in mind that the propeller will turn the sprocket gear clockwise during function. The arrow on the FS pattern of the gear indicates the direction it must turn during function.

Figure 12.08

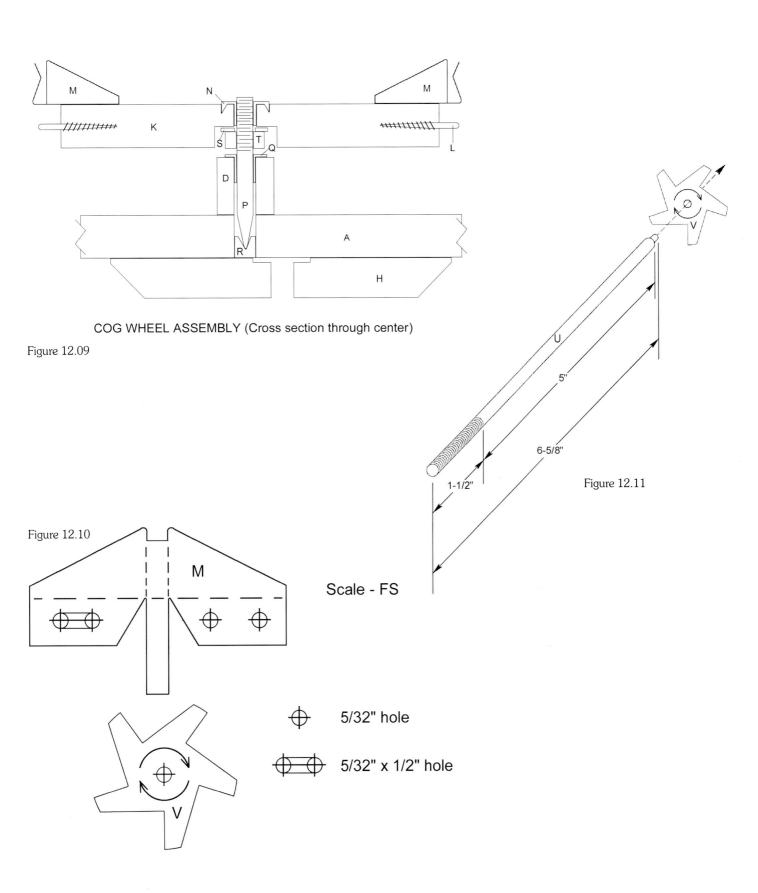

COG WHEEL ASSEMBLY (Cross section through center)

Figure 12.09

Figure 12.10

Figure 12.11

Scale - FS

5"

6-5/8"

1-1/2"

$\oplus$ 5/32" hole

$\oplus$ 5/32" x 1/2" hole

Fig. 12.12 shows the completed mechanical assembly, which must be adjusted to operate without jamming or jumping. By rearranging the distribution of the four spacer washers (W) on the drive shaft (U), the sprocket gear (V) can be positioned closer to or farther from the cogwheel. In addition, the cogwheel can be raised or lowered on the threaded end of the cogwheel pivot (P). By trial and error, the ideal combination of adjustments can be determined so that the mechanism will operate smoothly.

The pattern for the rudder is provided at FS/2 (Fig. 12.13). Enlarge the pattern to full size and secure it to a piece of .064" aluminum with spray adhesive. Cut out the rudder with a bandsaw or scroll saw. Use a wire wheel on a bench grinder to smooth the cut edges and prepare the surfaces of the metal for painting. Prime and paint the rudder as shown in Fig. 12.01.

Make a propeller for this whirligig with six 3-1/2" x 9" propeller blades as described in Chapter 1. Install a post pivot in the post pivot mounting block (H) as shown in Fig. 1.19. Make the stand and post as described in Chapter 1 (Figs. 1.03-1.06) of this book.

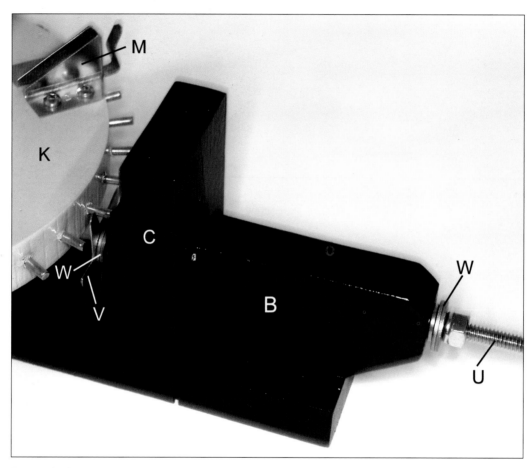

Figure 12.12

Chapter 13
Time and the Day

Time is the interval between successive events. The periods of light and darkness we experience and which reoccur on a regular basis are the events about which we organize our activities and rest. A day is the periodic event that is completed during the interval required for the earth to complete one revolution on its axis, producing a period of light and a period of darkness. Days have been arbitrarily divides into hours, minutes, and seconds and grouped into weeks and months. The day, however, is the most basic unit of time. This whirligig (Fig. 13.01) reproduces the events that occur during the period of one day. As the skyscape slowly turns, it displays sunrise, noon, sunset, and the night sky. The unique feature of this whirligig is its helical flange and cogwheel mechanism that produces the rota-

Figure 13.01

tion. Fig. 13.02 lists the parts and materials required to build this whirligig and will identify the parts labeled in all subsequent illustrations.

QTY	PART	NAME	DIMENSION (INCHES)			MATERIAL	NOTES
			T	W	L		
1	A	Chassis	3/4	2-1/2	19-1/2	Poplar or pine	Fig. 13.07
1	B	Drive shaft mtg. block	3/4	1/1/4	3	Poplar or pine	Fig. 13.06
1	C	Drive shaft end support	3/4	1-1/4	2-1/8	Poplar or pine	Fig. 13.06
1	D	Rudder	1/16	8	9-1/2	Aluminum	Fig. 13.07
2	E	Side panel	1/16	6-3/4	13	Aluminum	Fig. 13.07
2	F	Side panel spreaders	3/4 Diameter		2-1/2	Dowel	Fig. 13.05
1	G	Cog wheel	2	3 Diameter		Poplar or pine	
2	H	Cog wheel axle/washer	#8		1-1/4	SS/Brass screws	Fig. 13.03
22	J	Cog	#6 Size		1-1/2	Brass screws	
2	K	Skyscape disk	.064	12 Diameter		Aluminum	
1	L	Drive shaft	7/32 Diameter		10-1/4	Threaded brass rod	
1	M	Helical flange gear	.032	1-1/4 Diameter		Brass	Fig.13.04
1	N	Drive shaft stop	6-32 nut			Brass	
1	P	Propeller assembly	5-6 Blades				Fig. 1.03-1.06
1	Q	Post pivot assembly					Fig. 1.18
1	R	Stand					Fig. 1.22-1.24

TIME AND A DAY (Parts and materials)

Figure 13.02

The cylindrical cogwheel (G) has twenty-two cogs radially oriented and evenly spaced along its equator (Fig. 13.03). A helical flange on the drive shaft engages the cogs and rotates the cogwheel assembly. Use the technique outlined in Chapter 1, Cogwheels, to lay out the 3" diameter, 2" wide cogwheel for 22 cogs. Install the cogs (J) into predrilled pilot holes after the wheel has been painted. Each cog should extend 1/4" beyond the curved surface of the wheel.

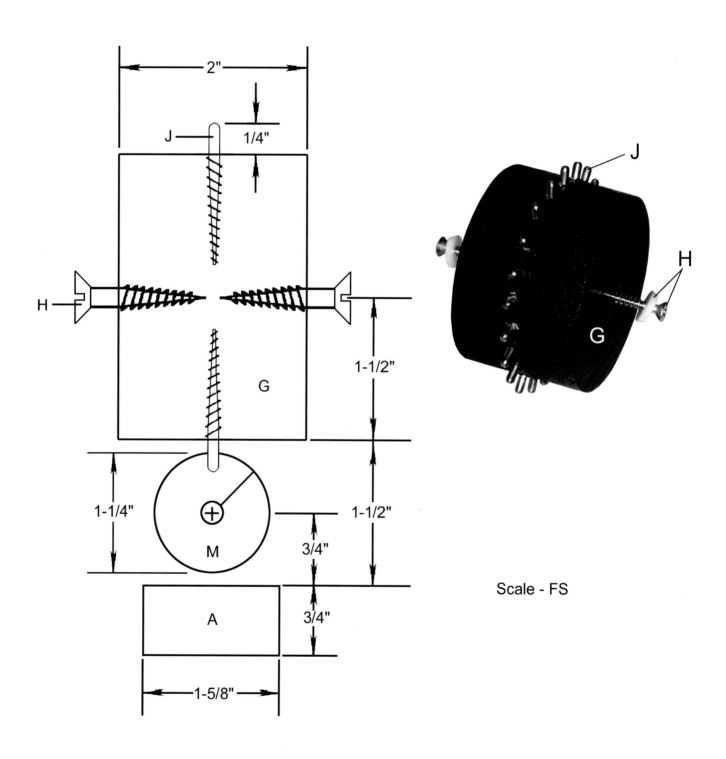

Scale - FS

Figure 13.03

Fig. 13.04 illustrates the drive shaft and helical flange gear assembly. Make the stop (N) from a 6-32 brass nut by enlarging the threaded hole to 7/32" diameter. Solder the stop on the shaft first, in the position shown on the diagram. Make the helical flange (M) from a disc of .032" brass 1-1/4" in diameter with a 7/32" hole in the center. Cut the disc from its perimeter to the center hole as shown on the FS pattern of this part. Bend the edges of the disc on either side of the cut away from each other until they are 1/2" apart at the perimeter. Solder the helical flange on the shaft in the position shown in the illustration.

Make the two skyscape disks (K) required from pieces of .064" x 12" x 12" aluminum. Locate and drill the center pilot holes for the #8 x 1-1/4" brass or SS flat head axle screws (H). Drill four equally spaced 5/32" holes on a 2" circle around the axle hole for the #6 x 5/8" screws to be used to join K to G. Paint K as shown in Fig. 13.01 before assembly with G.

The chassis assembly (Fig. 13.05) is comprised of parts A - F. FS patterns for B and C are provided in Fig. 13.06. A, D and E are shown as FS/2 in Fig. 13.07. Clearance holes and pilot holes for the screws used for assembling A - E are indicated on the patterns or plans for these parts. These positions must be accurately transferred and drilled if the joined parts are to align properly and the mechanism is to work without binding or jumping. Counterbore or countersink the holes in A for the screws to be used to attach B and C to A. If you intend to use bushings with the driveshaft, bore the driveshaft holes in B and C to match the outside diameter of the bushings. Paint all the parts before beginning assembly.

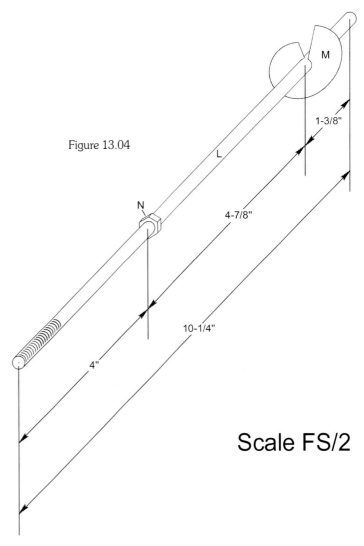

Figure 13.04

Scale FS/2

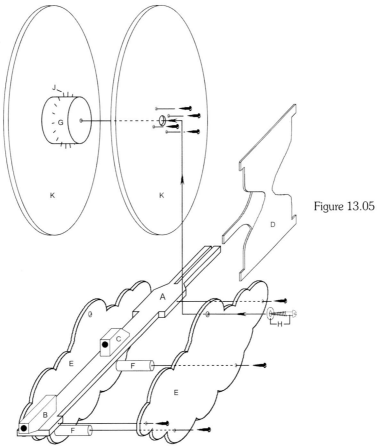

Figure 13.05

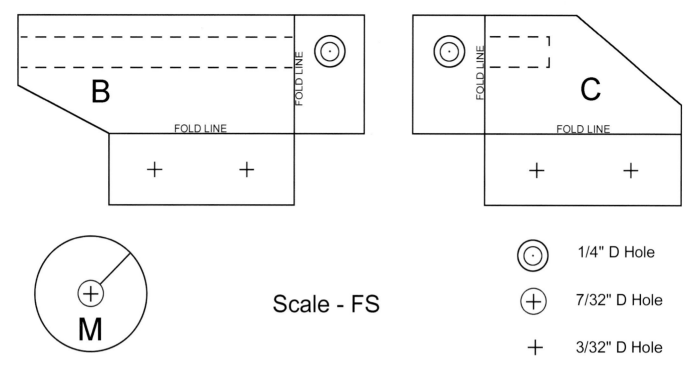

Scale - FS

◉ 1/4" D Hole

⊕ 7/32" D Hole

+ 3/32" D Hole

Figure 13.06

Install the driveshaft assembly between B and C before securing both parts to the chassis (A) with #6 x 1-1/4" SS FH screws (Fig. 13.08). Use #6 x 5/8" screws to secure the side panels (E) to the chassis (A) and the side panel spreaders (F). The oval holes in E will allow you to adjust the position of the cogwheel above the helical flange gear (M). Use external tooth SS washers under the heads of these mounting screws to attach E to A securely. Install the cogwheel assembly (G, J, K) between the side panels (E) using #8 x 1" stainless steel or brass wood screws (H) with nylon washers beneath their heads. Adjust the axle screws (H) to allow the entire cogwheel assembly to rotate freely.

Make a propeller with five or six 3-1/2" x 10" blades. See Chapter 1, Propellers, for details. Balance the propeller before painting. Assemble parts A-P and locate the balance point before installing the post-pivot assembly (Q).

Make a stand for your whirligig as described in Chapter 1 to complete this project.

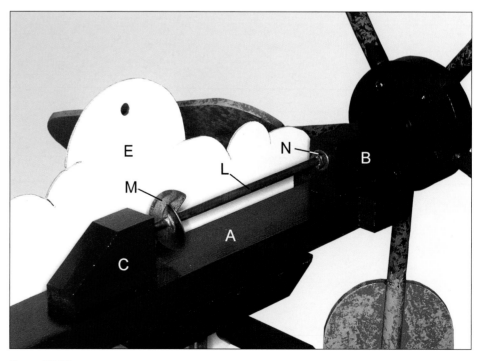

Figure 13.08

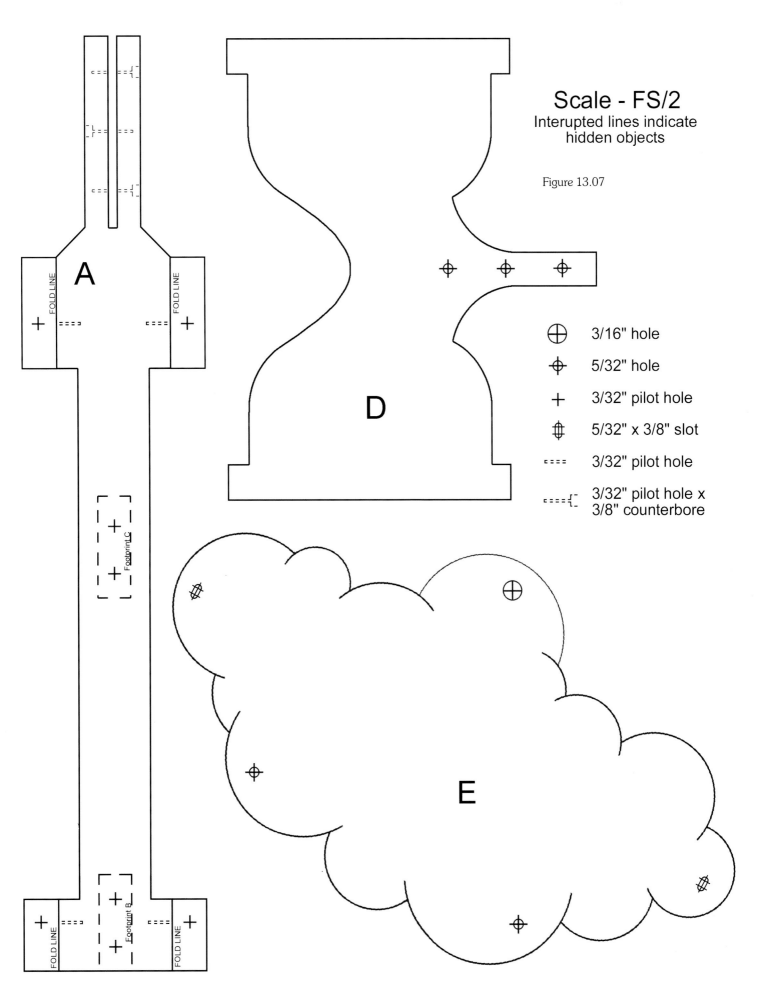

Scale - FS/2
Interupted lines indicate hidden objects

Figure 13.07

⊕   3/16" hole

⊕   5/32" hole

+   3/32" pilot hole

⊕   5/32" x 3/8" slot

⌐===   3/32" pilot hole

⌐===⌐   3/32" pilot hole x
          3/8" counterbore

A

FOLD LINE

FOLD LINE

Footprint C

Footprint B

FOLD LINE

FOLD LINE

D

E

Appendix

Materials, Supplies, and Tools

Aluminum half hard sheets I
Bearings
    Flanged bronze K
    Flanged nylon K
Brake B, C, D, J, L
Brass
    Rods C, J
    Screws C, J, K
    Sheet C, I, K
    Strips C, J
    Tubes C, J
Fasteners
    Brass screws C, J, K
    Stainless steel nuts, bolts, and washers A, H, K
    Stainless steel screws A, C, H, K
Lathe, metal mini B, C, D, J
Nibbler, metal C, D, J
Plaster cloth J
Pliers
    Sheet metal C, D
    3 prong F, G, J, M, O
Punch, portable hand C, D, J
Rivets and rivet tool C, D
Shears, metal bench B, C, D, J, L
Silver solder and flux F, G, M, O
Snips sheet metal hand C, D
Torch, butane F, J, M, O
Vise, multipositional E, J
Wood, mail order N

Vendors

A. Anchor Staple and Nail Company
    P.O. Box 570
    Wakefield RI 02880
    1-800-237 5555
    FAX 401-782-3762
    www.Anchorsssn.com

B. ENCO
    400 Nevada Pacific Hwy.
    Fernley, NV 89408
    1-800-873-3626
    FAX 1-800—965-5857
    www.Use-Enco.com

C. Grizzly Industrial Inc.
    P.O. Box 3110
    Bellingham, WA 98227-3110
    1-800-523-4777
    FAX 1-800-438-5901
    www.grizzley.com

D. Harbor Freight Tools
    3491 Mission Oaks Blvd
    P.O. Box 6010
    Camerillo, CA 93011-6010
    1-800-423-2567
    FAX 1-800-905-5220
    www.harborfreight.com

E. Leichtung Workshops
    1108 N Glenn Road
    Casper, WY 82601
    1-800-321-6840
    FAX 1-800-853-9663

F. Lincoln Dental Lab Supply Co.
    616 Hollywood Ave.
    Cherry Hill, NJ 08002
    1-800-289-6678
    FAX 609-663-3280
    www.lincolndental.com

G. Masel Orthodontic Supply Co.
    2701 Bartram Road
    Bristol, PA 19007
    1-800-423-8227

H. McFeely's Square Drive Screws
    3720 Cohen Place
    P.O. Box 11169
    Lynchburg, VA 24506-1169
    1-800-443-7937
    FAX 1-800-847-7136
    www.McFeelys.com

I. Metco Supply Company
    81 Kiski Ave.
    Leechburg, PA 15656
    1-412-842-3152
    1-800-521-8811
    www.metcosupply.com

J. Micro-Mark
    340 Snyder Ave.
    Berkeley Heights, NJ 07922-1595
    1-800-225-1066
    FAX 1-908-665-9383
    www.micromark.com

K. MSC Industrial Supply Co.
    151 Sunnyside Blvd.
    Plainview, NY 11803-9915
    1-800-645-7270
    FAX 1-800-255-5067
    www.MSCdirect.com

L. Northern Tool and Equipment Co.
    P.O. Box 1499
    Burnsville, MN 55337-0499
    1-800-553-5545
    FAX 1-612-894-0083
    www.northerntool.com

M. Pearson Dental
    13161 Telfair Ave.
    Sylmar, CA 91342
    1-800-336 8256
    FAX 818-833-3202
    www.pearsonlab.com

N. Steve Wall Lumber Co.
    P.O. Box 287
    Mayodan, NC 27027
    1-800-633-4062
    336-427 0637
    FAX 336-427-7588
    www.walllumber.com

O. Zahn Dental Laboratory Supply Co.
    135 Duryea Road
    Melville, NY 11747
    1-800-496-9500
    FAX 1-877-303-1100
    www.zahndental.com